Truthtellers of the Times

D1354394

Truthtellers of the Times

❧

Interviews with Contemporary Women Poets

Edited by Janet Palmer Mullaney

Introduction by Toi Derricotte

Ann Arbor

THE UNIVERSITY OF MICHIGAN PRESS

2001   2000   1999   1998   4   3   2   1

A CIP catalog record for this book is available from the British Library.

Library of Congress Cataloging-in-Publication Data

Truthtellers of the times : interviews with contemporary women poets /
edited by Janet Palmer Mullaney.
    p.   cm.
    Contents: Robin Becker — Gwendolyn Brooks — Lucille Clifton —
Lucha Corpi — Rita Dove — Joy Harjo — Josephine Jacobsen — June
Jordan — Janice Mirikitani — Alicia Ostriker — Linda Pastan —
Minnie Bruce Pratt — May Miller Sullivan — Karen Swenson.
    ISBN 0-472-09680-X (cloth : alk. paper). — ISBN 0-472-06680-3
(paper : alk. paper)
    1. Women poets, American—20th century—Interviews.   2. American
poetry—Women authors—History and criticism—Theory, etc.
3. American poetry—20th century—History and criticism—Theory,
etc.   4. Women and literature—United States.   5. Poetry—
Authorship.   I. Mullaney, Janet Palmer.
PS151.T78   1998
811'.54099287—dc21   98-21815
                                                           CIP

Contents

Introduction

by Toi Derricotte

I am teaching for a week at Flight of the Mind, a workshop retreat outside Eugene, Oregon, for women writers. Founded by Judith Barrington and Ruth Gundle fifteen years ago, the retreat is held at a rustic monastery beside the beautiful McKenzie River, whose shining aquamarine waters rush down over silk-black rocks. At night, lying parallel to its roar, I sleep and am dreamless, and the river enters the soles of my feet, courses through my whole body as if it were a channel, until everything in me that blocks its path is aligned with the river's pouring. This morning one of the women in class, a physician, said, "The act of writing actually changes one's mind, changes the neurons and chemistry."

For example, I begin writing this introduction on the back of a letter written to me by one of the women in the group. I've been having a hard time beginning, and I believe that her words, what she says with an open and generous heart on one side of this paper, are connected to, permit, stimulate, infuse, give heart, breath, current to me on this other side—untranslated and untranslatable what is between us, but necessary to what I need to say. My brain grows dull, there is a gap in feeling, maybe I'm afraid. Somehow in the middle of what we can't do, we are giving each other support and permission, so that what we can't or shouldn't do gets done. We *are* changing. Janet Palmer Mullaney's remarkable collection is a tribute to that change. It not only admits it, it is, indeed, constructed to address it and, perhaps, can even be read as a guidebook to its crossing.

The most striking attribute of this collection is its diversity.

Herein speak poets gay and straight, of various ages, ethnicities, lifestyles and aesthetic persuasions, traditional and non-traditional. You might think that a group with such far flung geographic and cultural centers would suggest that there is no longer any common ground in American poetry. Quite to the contrary, this collection shows a surprising agreement among the poets about the most important characteristics of writing and a writer's life. It makes evident an invisible network, a community that, though not formally joined, is meaningfully allied in its purpose.

For most of the poets in this collection, the project of twentieth- and twenty-first-century literature is one of change. This includes artistic change, but extends beyond poetry into life. Minnie Bruce Pratt says, "I think the concept of writing or art as just self-expression or self fulfillment is a Eurocentric and sterile patriarchal idea. . . . You are able to make art only because things come to you from your community. The image of the individualistic egocentric artist— white, male, and heterosexual—is premised on him creating all by himself in defiance of his culture."

Though a few poets do not speak directly of change in their interviews, nevertheless, it is evident in their work. At the very least, all of the poets have a keen awareness of the effects of oppression. Josephine Jacobsen states, "Being oppressed in America, whether it's black people or women, inevitably breeds a lack of self-confidence, an ambivalence about success. . . . What has happened is because of the assumptions that women had no intellectual capacity and that there was nowhere for them to go if they had. God knows how many silent poets went to the grave because being a poet was not a practical, emotional, or mental option."

Many poets speak of courageous choices their work has led them to make. Gwendolyn Brooks says, "Publishing with a black press is a statement on my part. . . . I'm not going back to other presses, even if I have to publish my books myself." Janice Mirikitani speaks about how her writing moves her both outward and inward, to painful confrontations with the self:

What affects my writing at this point are some of the women's programs I helped create. We don't deal with recovery as an isolated issue.... You have to address the racism, the childhood abuses, the feelings of rejection and worthlessness. We started groups for many different areas of abuse. As part of that, I had to face my own incestuous childhood and to admit my own addictions to powerlessness, self-hate, and self-destructiveness, the circle of recovering women constantly forces me to face myself and what I have to do.

A surprising number of the poets speak of the importance of addressing the spiritual aspect of our nature. This may require us to develop different ways of sensing. The poetry of women of color has been essential in this regard, and, thank God, Ms. Mullaney's editorial choices gives them credit. Joy Harjo says, "The supernatural world is ingrained in our culture, and it is another way of knowing.... In European culture, the world is supposed to have three dimensions, and it's constructed in a way that only the five senses can maneuver. There are probably more than five senses; there are probably ten, twelve, a hundred senses, which we haven't developed." Lucille Clifton speaks of the non-linear, perhaps even subversive, aspects of change. "Kali had—we all have—many sides. She was both destroyer and creator, and it's always been interesting me to me that she was black. And it is possible for me to, for people, to be both creator and destroyer. I tell my students all the time that 'both/and' is an African-American tradition, not 'either-or.' "

Many of the writers speak about being between homes, if not literal homes, then not having the supports of their usual or expected communities. Karen Swenson says, "Being alien magnificently wrenches me out of my culture, gives me a chance to view what we take for granted as much as breathing, to see it from a different perspective, test its values, see if I agree."

I took on the writing of this introduction at a time when I was in the middle of enormous changes in my own personal and professional life. I had just published two books, one of which, a memoir, *The Black Notebooks,* took twenty-five years to write. I had gone through the devastating end of a love relationship. Overwhelming commitments made it almost impossible to write. I needed to hear from other poets, to hear how they had survived loss, what things they believed in and worked for, what things kept their hearts alive.

I found this: the presence of a larger network of support, a basis and ground for all of our work, a mysterious connection between us that nourishes us through difficult times and gives us the courage and willingness to make change, an optimism and joy to be part of this meaningful labor. "I don't think that a poet can separate herself or himself from the world," Joy Harjo says. "We are charged with being truthtellers of the times. This is true for any poet in any culture. I have done other kinds of writing, but poetry demands the truth, and you cannot separate the poem from your political reality. It's a continuum." "The truth" always resists arriving at a point. In Ms. Mullaney's collection, it is characterized by a dignified balance, complicated, delicate, and, shall I say, feminine?

Robin Becker

Robin Becker was born in Philadelphia in 1951. She has received awards from the National Endowment for the Arts and the Massachusetts Artists Foundation. Her poems are widely published and appear in various publications such as *The American Poetry Review,* and she is the Poetry Editor of *The Women's Review of Books*. Her most recent book, *All-American Girl* (1996), was nominated for the 1996 Lambda Literary Award. Other books include *Giacometti's Dog* (1990), *Backtalk* (1982), and *Personal Effects* (1976). Becker currently teaches at Pennsylvania State University.

All-American Girl, *the title of your recent book of poetry, seems to play a bit with our notions of "all-American." You are a Jewish lesbian—the granddaughter of a woman transplanted from Russia to the United States. What role does religion play in your life?*

I don't attend synagogue or have Jewish religious practices such as Friday night Sabbath, nor do I have private or individual Jewish practices as part of my daily life. However, when I moved from Cambridge to State College, Pennsylvania, I felt a longing to be around Jews. So I found a Community Center there. My presence at the Jewish Community Center includes a Bar Mitzvah of a colleague's child and two High Holiday Services.

I think about joining the center and participating more vigorously, yet each time I decide not to. At this point I haven't found a way to bring structured Jewish practices into my life.

That seems true for many people: yearning to be part of a community but feeling that one can't quite fit.

Maybe I would feel more motivated if there were a group of Gay and Lesbian Jews affiliated with the synagogue, because my Jewish self is intertwined with those identities. I feel that my feminist and lesbian selves are not visible there: I'm seen as a middle-class Ashkenazi Jewish woman. And that feels like only one segment of what I am.

Is that different—or the same—in your poems?

The privacy and solitude of the cabin where I write allow for a kind of integration that just isn't possible in one's daily life. As a Jew, as a lesbian, as a feminist, as someone fighting against breast cancer, I am an activist. It's important to march for safe streets for women. At the same time, I feel that the only way I can pull it all together is in the poems, where more of a sense of wholeness is possible. What makes them possible is a withdrawal from participation.

Three poems, "The Crypto-Jews," "Dreaming at the Rexall Drug," and "Family Romance," are marked by a sense of travel—of leaving and returning to the same place but in a different way.

Interesting. That's in line with a *New Yorker* essay I just read by Jamaica Kincaid, in which she said that one needs to leave home in order to write well and think clearly.

To grow, to understand more deeply, we must leave our places of origin. The Russian grandmother leaves home in "Dreaming at the Rexall Drug." The two women stuck with a dilemma about whether to have children in "Family Romance" leave the place that they have selected. The Jews—to survive—leave.

Is that theme conscious for you, or did it emerge from writing the poems?

Like many people, I had to leave to survive an oppressive family situation. I literally took flight; my sister took her own life. So, I think the flight impulse is old and deep in me, as it is in many creative artists. Your way to hear your own voice, see your own vision, hear your own music, is to get out, early. That impulse gets in the bones.

The central fact of being lesbian and Jewish grounds the poems in All-American Girl *in a wonderful specificity. Do your poems reach beyond those specifics?*

Many people will read them who haven't lost a sister to suicide or who are not Jewish; I hope the poems resonate in terms of a loss. I also hope they speak to non-Jews who wish to understand what it is to be a Jew in a Christian country.

In what ways does religion intersect with or diverge from sexual identity in your poems?

When I was researching for "The Horse Fair," I discovered that Rosa Bonheur, a French painter who had a long and abiding commitment to one woman for forty years, had difficulty managing her lesbian identity in French society of the 1840s and 1850s.

In order to visit slaughterhouses and horse fairs, Bonheur had to get permission from the French government to dress in men's clothes so that she wouldn't be harassed. There was already prejudice against her for being an "anamalier"—a woman who painted in a man's domain. She won a commission from the government to do a painting to celebrate French agriculture. "Why should a woman have this opportunity?" many people wondered. "Who was she muscling in on such a powerful subject?" One way to put Bonheur down was to accuse her of being a Jew. Since *Bonheur* means "good hour" and *Mazel-Tov* means "congratulations," they teased her in print by calling her "Rosa Mazel-Tov." The conflation in the minds of French society of her lesbianism with Judaism is an example of further marginalization.

That discovery must have been shocking.

I was so shocked that I quote it in the center of the poem. There was so much anti-Semitism in France that it was just one of the weapons that you took out. There wasn't institutionalized homophobia, as we have it, so much as an institutionalized anti-Semitism.

In what ways do you use myths in your new, longer poems? And how does that differ from your work in All-American Girl?

Recently, during the High Holidays, my ex-girlfriend gave birth to the child I refused to stay with her and parent. I went to Harvard's Hillel and spent days going between the services—where I heard the beautiful passages of Hebrew I've listened to once a year all my life—and the hospital, where my ex-girlfriend was with her new partner and baby. I felt somewhat marginal at the services and *very* marginal at the hospital. So, I decided to work on a poem that would integrate these two experiences.

"Days of Awe" borrows from the High Holiday text and uses narratives from the Old Testament. (The baby's name is Joseph, so I use the story of Joseph and the coat of many colors.) I allowed myself a freedom to juxtapose myths with events that is not present in my other poems. I let the reader make leaps with me.

Tell me more about that.

I don't create hinges between the quotations from the prayerbook and the speaker who is in the hospital: I let the reader kind of "run behind." Usually, I like to feel that the reader and I are marching together, but here I take risks. I attribute this to having a whole year to write.

The fiction writer Raymond Carver once said, upon being asked why he wrote short stories, that he didn't have time to write longer ones because he had to work and had children. But you were able to move into these larger forms.

Yes, and now I'm very interested in them. I'm writing a long poem on a painter who was killed in the Holocaust, Charlotte Solomon. She died at twenty-six, hiding in France. Seven people in her family committed suicide, so there's a connection for me to the arts, to Judaism, and to suicide. The complete collection of her paintings is in Amsterdam. Her family knew the Franks, so Anne and Charlotte's fathers were conscious of inheriting the arts of their nonsurviving daughters.

Charlotte painted her aunt jumping out of a window saying, "I can't bear it any more, I'm so alone." She did very quirky paintings.

What can you say about your time at the Bunting Institute of Radcliffe College?

It is so important—particularly for women in the middle of their professional lives—to have time to reflect and pause. I was given a great gift this year of time to spend in the company of such women. Like everyone else, we are often unable to see the larger design or to see ourselves in it.

For some people being at the institute meant time to reconsider: to leave the academy, to veer off in a different direction, to relocate. It serves lots of different purposes. For women who are in the academy, especially, this is one way to get yourself back.

(1996)

Gwendolyn Brooks

Gwendolyn Brooks was born in Topeka, Kansas, in 1917. By the age of sixteen, she had already published over seventy poems. Brooks was the first African American to win the Pulitzer Prize (*Annie Allen,* 1950). She is known for her use of colloquial speech and her portrayal of poor, urban African Americans. She has been awarded over fifty honorary doctorates, has won two Guggenheim Fellowships, has served as Poetry Consultant to the Library of Congress (1985–86), and was Poet Laureate of Illinois in 1968. Some of her best-known works include *Annie Allen* (1949), *The Bean Eaters* (1960), *Riot* (1969), *Family Pictures* (1970), and *To Disembark* (1981). She has also published children's literature and poetry, novels, and an autobiography.

Visiting Gwendolyn Brooks in her Washington office, I immediately detected evidence of a burgeoning black presence. The Library of Congress is full of the likes of Wordsworth, Emerson, and Yeats, but there on the overflow table beside her desk is a treasured volume of poems by Langston Hughes and books by contemporary black poets. They rest patiently, awaiting the exposure that Gwen Brooks will surely bestow upon them in her undertakings as the twenty-ninth (and first black woman) poetry consultant.

The image of this demure woman with the short salt-and-pepper Afro reminds me of a drawing of the eighteenth-century black poet Phyllis Wheatley. I see the same brooding pensiveness, the famous downturned smile-frown, the extended finger pressed deeply into the dark, full cheeks. Brooks sits solemnly, her back rigid against the chair, but the brilliance of the flames that dance in her eyes conquers her decorum. I remind myself that this is no "hey-girl-what's-happenin" sister I will be talking with. This is Gwendolyn Brooks. Oak. Fine, mellowed wine.

Brooks's first book was published in 1945. Her appointment as the "congressional poet laureate" (my own term) comes forty years after she had launched her writing career, hoping, as she told me, she could have just one book published. To date there have been seventeen. She has published many works of poetry, a novel, books for children, and part 1 of an autobiography (pt. 2 is forthcoming).

"This is a 'working' award," she chuckles, emphasizing the word *working,* "and they have quite a few things for me to do here. When poets come to be recorded, I will supervise that. I'll be having what I call 'reading lunches'—a couple of poets right here in this office, with teensy-weensy audiences and bag lunches."

"But I must remind you that I'm a consultant, not a commander!" She booms out her words for effect. "I am not in charge of the Library of Congress!"

"If," she continues, in a manner that reveals both the diplomacy and indomitability of a professional, "if I know of anybody that I think is singularly deserving, I can recommend them." She names several poets, black and white, significant and unknown. "I certainly want to introduce children to poetry. People really underrate children's talent. I think the audience will be amazed at what these kids can do by way of writing and also by way of presenting themselves. It's going to be a lot of fun and also rewarding."

At sixty-eight this Pulitzer Prize–winning, Illinois poet laureate still pays homage to her roots, and she speaks of strong ones. She attributes her passion for literature and her appreciation for "the things of life that are called little" to devoted parents who nurtured their children's interests, even through the mean years of the Depression in Chicago. Brooks's mother, upon discovering that her daughter wanted to be a writer, was determined that young Gwen would be the "Lady Paul Laurence Dunbar."

"That's what she said. She said I was going to be a poet!" Brooks leans forward, and her look says, "What can you do when your mama tells you that?" Her laughter bubbles gently, like soup that is almost done and boiling happily in the pot. "I was lucky to have parents who loved literature. We always had a lot of books. I used to read especially Emerson's essays, poetry, and fairy tales— not necessarily in that order."

She reflects on the gifts of her father: a bookcase bought as a wedding present for her mother, a set of Harvard Classics purchased before the birth of his children ("because he knew he would have a family"). He had aspired to become a doctor yet accepted janitor's overalls in order to feed his family. He was a man who recited poetry to his children and whom she overwhelmingly remembers as being kind.

In all, Brooks recalls, "They were common folk. They came from nice people" (*nice* is extended and given a graceful lilt), "people who were decent, who liked to be clean. They went to church. They loved baking pies, cornbread, navy beans, and ham hocks." Her next words are shot out in a tight stream: "They were or-di-nar-y people, not people who put on airs. I hate that with a passion—people who think they are too good for their own folk!"

It was the poet Langston Hughes whom she credits for vivifying this beauty of common folk of color. "He had the kind of spirit I have. That's why black people loved him, even through the late 1960s, when they were busy flushing everything 'irrelevant'!"

I ask her if she feels that today's black writers have lost the common touch. She responds resolutely: "No, I can't think of a black poet who doesn't deal with the 'hoi polloi.' We have a poet like Audre Lorde, who is very introspective, but even her springboard is ordinary black people. Mari Evans, Haki (Madhubuti), definitely Sonia Sanchez, Nikki Giovanni—they deal with ordinary people doing ordinary things in extraordinary situations."

Still, she has some reservations. To Brooks blackness still counts. She stands like a sentry, the alert elder who reminds us of a time when we capitalized the word out of respect and when its impact on our psyches was far more concrete. "I think we're dealing with what we ought to deal with," she says and then pauses and reflects quietly. Then she implores, "I would like some of us to be a little blacker."

Brooks believes that integration and assimilation have heightened, rather than lessened, the disparities between blacks and whites and among blacks themselves. "It's a peculiar time, with so much emphasis on riches. Black folks look at TV and see "Dynasty" and "Dallas," and they see these high-fallutin' ways of living. Sometimes they take their blackness and sit on it. I think the general reaction has been to resent and covet at the same time."

She searches for a poem that speaks to her observation and finds it in "A Man of the Middle Class." The poem unravels the frustration of a black man who strives to enter the mainstream by acquiring the material possessions that he resents the whites for having. "He's defected his essential blackness. He has deprived himself of some real nourishment so that he can identify more with the larger culture. He asks, 'But have I answers?' and recognizes that whites haven't found any answers to demonstrate that they're superior either."

She relates an experience at Wellesley College earlier this year: "I was reading, and a young black girl, about my color, was sitting over near the very edge, listening very carefully. When I got through she said, 'I want to say something to you. Why do you keep talking about blackness? I don't want to hear this. The time for that is over. We are now Americans, and that is all I want to be.' "

"Well," Brooks gapes, "my mouth hung open! But it shouldn't

have, because there's a lot of that kind of feeling. I can't tell you how many times people do that to me!" She grins, claps her hands, and rocks back and forth in her chair. "We really have a lot of mess, don't we?"

Today's renewed interest in the writing of black women, Brooks feels, has brought attention once again to her novel, *Maud Martha,* but she does not believe that her works have been sought out as primarily "women's writing." She has never seen her woman's vision as a separate one. As she says, "I've never belonged to that Ms. group of black, or white, women writers." Yet, although Brooks may not write with feminist intent, her female voices speak with a conviction that enables them to rise above the rigid confines of what is often deemed, even in the black experience, a woman's place. Her women are assertive, conscious people who battle "isms" in ways that are consistent with their experience. Like Brooks herself, they defy subordination and reconstruct their own aesthetic in an often hostile, ugly world.

I sense, though, that Brooks is listening intently to what is in the wind. As a poet, she has always placed herself and her poetry effectively. She has uplifted many voices that were previously unheralded. "If any of those women are interested in black family, and when I say that I'm talking about the whole of black commitment, I certainly am with them in spirit. And with them, if need be, if they are interested in furthering their own strengths and influence."

Brooks remains adamant about publishing only with a black press, which she has done since the mid-1960s, even though her experience with the financially troubled Broadside Press in Detroit has resulted in some of her works becoming unavailable. "Publishing with a black press is a statement on my part. What we need, of course, is more black publishing companies. I know that a lot of them are gone now; they were not able to stay in business because of money. But I'm not going back to other presses, even if I have to publish my books myself."

I ask if she would consider publishing with a black or Third World women's press such as Kitchen Table: Women of Color Press. Brooks is only remotely aware of KTP's existence, but she expresses interest in learning more about such outfits. "But I don't like the idea of having a lot of publishers. It's hard enough, psychologically, having one! Besides, I've been perfectly happy with Third World Press."

Gwendolyn Brooks was given exceptional feature coverage in the major Washington papers prior to her inaugural appearance at the Library of Congress. On that night she was received by an enraptured audience that had waited, good-naturedly, some for more than two hours, for the auditorium doors to open. The mood of the crowd, which was composed of blacks and whites of diverse backgrounds, could be compared to the euphoria that blacks shared upon Joe Louis's 1937 title bout victory. Five hundred or so lucky people were seated. Three hundred more viewed the reading on a video screen in an adjacent room. Two hundred more were turned away, and they left only reluctantly.

The literati and the common folk received her. Book collectors and book borrowers alike awaited the opportunity to greet her. We listened and responded to this woman, whose reading of her own work was titillating, dramatic, sometimes explosive, often comic. The undeniable magnetism of Gwendolyn Brooks pulled us all closer together. And, when the literary smoke cleared that night, black literature, women's literature—indeed, the whole body of fine letters—had no steadier beacon than her. It was she who exited the ring undiminished, champion of the long, tough rounds of polemics and poetics. Like her endearing character Lincoln West, Gwendolyn Brooks remains "the real thing."

(1986)

Photo by Michael S. Glaser

Lucille Clifton

Lucille Sayles Clifton was born in 1936 in Depew, New York. Clifton's parents were uneducated blue-collar workers who appreciated literature—her mother wrote poetry and her father was an avid storyteller. Her first book, *Good Times: Poems* (1969), was cited as one of the best books of the year by the *New York Times*. In 1988 Clifton was the first author to have two books (*Good Woman* and *Next*) chosen as finalists for the Pulitzer Prize. She has been Poet Laureate of Maryland and has won grants from the National Endowment for the Arts. Clifton is known for her portrayal of African-American youth and family life, and her work often addresses political and religious themes. She has also written an autobiography and many children's books.

You have said that if the officers of the LA Police Department had been readers of poetry, they couldn't have beaten Rodney King.

I am certain. They couldn't have done it so easily because poetry allows you to see beyond yourself, to try to reach toward the sameness in the other.

In a way fiction doesn't?

It may be that poetry goes more directly to the inside. The brain and intellect start you thinking too much. Poetry seeks different ways of seeing and understanding, something beyond the self and larger than the sum of its parts. And that allows us to understand that humans also are larger than the sum of all their parts.

Poetry seems to have always been part of your life. In Generations *it sounded as if you knew you wanted to be a poet from the time you were a teenager.*

When I was a little girl, writing poems just came to me because I read a lot and loved the magical sound and music of language. It never occurred to me to say I wanted to be a poet. What seemed possible was being a nurse, being a teacher, or marrying a preacher. I wasn't going to do any of that! What was true about me was that I could breathe and I "made" poems. But I never thought of having a career as a poet.

What was your poetry like when you started writing?

Traditional. I loved Edna St. Vincent Millay's sonnets, and I started writing sonnets and trying to use the language as best I could. By the time I was first published I had been writing with major intent for more than twenty years. Not the intent of publishing, which is what it often is today, but attempting to serve the poem well.

You hadn't thought of trying to publish your work?

You must remember that I was born in 1936 near Buffalo, New York. The only poets I ever saw or heard of were the portraits that hung on the walls of my elementary school—old dead white men from New England with beards. Of course, it didn't seem to be a possibility for me. It's important to remember that writing and publishing poems are two different things.

Who encouraged you as a writer?

No one. I was not *dis*couraged. My parents encouraged me in that they always said I could do anything I wanted to. I didn't know any other writers when I first started. I never took creative writing classes or workshops. I think it's important to say that these days.

What in your home environment went into your becoming a writer?

We were verbal people, and my parents were great readers, although neither one finished elementary school. My father could read but not write. I always say my literary antecedent was Reverend Merriweather from the Macedonia Baptist Church because of his oratory.

I hear the rhythms of the Bible in a lot of your poems.

Do you? I'll have to look for that now. I used to hear my father (who is a great Bible person) and my grandmother read the Bible. I reveled in the roll of the language, especially the King James version. The Bible must be there somewhere, because poetry comes out of all that we are, and part of what I am is someone who attended church regularly as a child. My father was Southern Baptist, and my mother was Sanctified, which is a holy roller–type religion. The church influenced me, perhaps not as much in subject matter as in energy. It's a mistake to think that we are products of what we are taught. We are products of all that we learn and some of what we are taught. I, as a child surrounded on Sunday by the vibrations of a Baptist church, must have absorbed something.

How does your spirituality relate to your writing now?

People say all the time that I'm a religious poet, although I'm not a particularly religious person. I do think I'm spiritual. I remember the day I first said to my father, "I don't think I want to go to church today." He was shocked—he didn't know how to deal with it. I'm fond of sacred places but don't like to worship in them; I always say I want to live in one. I used to visit churches, and I go to Seder; a good friend who was a priest used to take me to cathedrals. I've been to lots of different kinds of rituals, but I don't hang with any particular one.

I married a philosopher. Toward the end of his life, if you asked my husband what he did, he would say he was a mystic. And I think he was. He did yogic practices and was interested in Eastern belief systems and traveled to India, to Tibet, to Africa.

Your sequence of poems called "The Light That Came to Lucille Clifton" seems to reflect a mystical experience.

It does. The poems reflect a kind of otherness that has been with me most of my life. I decided to write them after I heard another poet say, "It's funny I don't know much about Lucille's inner life."

So it wasn't a one-time experience but something you have experienced frequently?

Yes. The poems are pretty literal, actually.

Do you hear a voice?

Yes, I do hear voices. It's the kind of thing that's hard to explain if a person hasn't had it. An awareness of otherness has always been in my life. I accept that as I accept the rest of who I am. It doesn't get in my way.

Do you feel it's the voice of God?

No, it's just an awareness of more than the physical. Many people have that and don't quite know what to call it. They talk about hunches, intuitions; well, I have them a lot and have learned to heed them and incorporate them into my living.

And you sometimes experience your intuition as a light or a vision?

I use *light* a lot in my writing. *Lucille* means "light," and it takes on various meanings: *The Book of Light* is about clearness, seeing things whole, seeing what's there and more.

Many of your poems retell Bible characters' stories in their own words.

Well, I'll speak for anybody! I wanted to find the humanity in their stories. Someone said to me once that I find the myth in the human and the human in the myth. In the new book I speak for Leda, for Atlas, for Naomi in the Bible. I always say I speak in the voices of the living *and* the dead. To feel yourself into another is what poetry can do for us, and I think I'm not bad at it. That doesn't make the stories less sacred or divine; it makes them more so to me. It is much more wonderful and miraculous to know that a poor peasant girl did something than to know that an angel did it. And I like to tell the stories: I like the Seder idea of keeping our stories known. If we know stories, we can understand more about what being human is.

In your poems and in Generations *you've told the story of your own family, going back to when your great-great-grandmother was brought from Africa as a slave.*

My father told those stories to me over and over. That made them seem important. He told them to whoever was present, but I listened. We must preserve the past for the future's sake. If we see our lives as an ongoing story, it's important to include all the ingredients and not have it in little compartments. I like to think of it not as "that was then, this is now" but that they all connect. For some reason I've always found the stories between the stories more interesting, wondered the hows and the whys to things. What has gone into making us who we are? Is it good or not? What is destroying us? What will keep us warm?

You seem to have a special fascination with the story of Mary.

I do like Mary, don't I? I'm fond of her.

But you seem ambivalent about whether her story is blessed or horrible.

I wonder what she thinks! I should think for her it was a mixed blessing. I think her mother, Anna, would fight this. I would, if my daughter said "Mom, I hear voices telling me I'm about to get pregnant and my kid's going to hang on a tree." I would probably say, "We will not hear this; we won't listen to that again; we will not watch the stars." I'll bet Anna wanted for her child what I want for mine: happiness, peace, some kind of family life as she defines it.

You also seem to have a fascination with the Hindu goddess Kali.

People tell me: "Lucille, you're always happy. You've always been happy. You've never had a bad time. You're always smiling." Well, how would they know? I smile a lot, and I have a sense of humor. Things happen to be very funny. But Kali had—we all have—many sides. She was both destroyer and creator, and it's always been interesting to me that she was black. And it is possible for me, too, for people, to be both creator and destroyer. I tell my students all the time that "both/and" is an African-American tradition, not "either-or."

How did you start writing children's books?

I've been publishing them as long as I've been publishing poetry. A children's book and *Good Times* were both published in 1969. I was friends with Maxine Kumin—who wrote children's books with Anne Sexton—and we worked together on a project for the Department of Education years ago. Maxine suggested that, because I have so many kids, I might try a children's book, and I found that I could. I must have been waiting to do it for a long time, although I'd never expressed that desire, because *Some of the Days of Everett Anderson* took about half an hour to write down!

You've written a series of Everett Anderson books. How did you create his character?

I wanted to write a book about a child from the projects to show that being materially poor doesn't mean being poor in spirit. Even in those days there was a tendency for girls to defer to boys in the black community. My mother didn't finish school so her brothers could go, for instance. Later, somebody pointed out that I'd written about boys all the time—I'd never noticed—so I started writing about girls, too.

Bantam has reissued seven of my children's books, including *The Black ABCs*, which has a verse for every letter, starting with "*A* is for Africa, land of the sun, the king of continents, the mighty one." I then talk about Africa having so many different languages, some of the world's largest rivers, and so on. I like that book because of my *X*; in those days *X* in the alphabet was always a xylophone. My *X* is for Malcolm. I was pleased to have thought of that in 1970!

I heard you say at a conference several years ago that having six children was the best thing that ever happened to your writing.

It kept me human and kept my priorities absolutely together. People are more important than things, and I know it. Kids don't let you be elitist or take yourself too seriously. They teach you all kinds of things: patience, turns of phrase, that you can handle more than you think you can, that things are never lost. To care for something besides yourself, to take yourself out of the center of your doing. I learned that there were a lot of things I didn't have to do. I learned how to keep things in my head. So, when I sit down to write, I'm not just starting: A lot has already happened.

How did you write when your children were small?

My earlier poems are shorter than my later ones, if you notice. But I can write and do other things at the same time. Everybody who has kids knows that. Somebody asked me once, "What are the optimum circumstances under which you write?" When you're in the kitchen and four of the kids have measles. One learns that one's process is what it has to be.

These kinds of questions are wonderings from the academy. It's as if poetry started there. But poetry didn't start at a desk or at a computer. The first poem came from somebody walking out of a cave somewhere and looking up and seeing the stars and saying wow! My poems are wow! Poetry is not completely an intellectual activity. Nor is it wise to think that what we wish to be is intellectuals. I am not one. Poems come out of human lives, human activities.

Is it ever hard for you being part of the academy?

I've entered the academy, but I don't put on all the academy's clothes. Mostly because I can't get very many of them on! Sometimes my feelings are hurt when I think what I do is underrated by some people, especially because they know I didn't graduate from a four-year college. But I'm good at ignoring what I feel like ignoring, and I'm grounded in myself. One of the blessings of being born an African-American woman is that I learned a long time ago not to buy other people's definitions of who I am and what I'm supposed to be like.

I've never felt that I had to limit myself in any way to be part of the academy. It is there to serve students, and I'm interested in that. I don't do a whole lot of other foolishness.

Do you have any thoughts about how poetry is taught to children?

It is taught badly in school because it's taught by people who were taught badly. People fear it. Teachers have asked me about when children are ready to learn poems, but children love the music of language. I don't presume to know what a particular child is able to understand. Some things we enjoy whether we understand them or not—like *Jabberwocky*. One of the first things I remember reading was *The Citadel* by A. J. Cronin. I was about five. I didn't know what a citadel was, but I loved the word. I got something out of it. Poetry needs to be taught, even on college campuses, because it is something that can be loved. When you hear people talk about literature, they often do not talk about that reason for it. But often we are taught that this is what a civilized person needs to know.

We have so many stereotypes about what is possible for certain kinds of people to know. So that if some folks are poor they can't know Leninism; they would not enjoy Bach. I had a student once who turned in poetry by Emily Dickinson because she thought I would only know Nikki Giovanni. The idea that I wouldn't know the world of American poetry!

Many of your poems deal with the danger of nature being destroyed.

If you're interested in life, you have to be interested in all of it, and, if you're concerned about life and its well-being, you have to be concerned even with life that does not look like oneself.

In the poem "Being Property Myself Once" and many others you make a connection between destruction of earth and oppression of people, especially minorities.

One has to see it as connected. When I think about property, how can I not associate it with coming from a line of people who were considered property? My problem—or my gift—is to have a long memory.

"The Killing of the Trees" connects destroying trees with the destruction of Native Americans.

I wrote that poem when I first moved to St. Mary's County [Md.]. I lived in a new development and had just come from California, where cutting down trees for no reason is just not done. But men were cutting down trees as if it were something wonderful; there seemed to be no feeling for preserving the landscape. And the tree did for a moment flash in my eyes as if it were a warrior chief.

Native American culture comes up in a lot of your poems.

I've always been interested in our misuse of Native American names. "They Are Afraid of Her" was the name of Crazy Horse's daughter. One man's name really translates into English as "Young Man Who Is So Fierce Even His Horses Are Fierce," yet he was called Young Man Afraid of His Horses. Isn't that awful? It's terrible to do that. Crazy Horse's native name translates as "Young Man Whose Horses Dance under Him as If They Were Enchanted." To trivialize history, including the stories and practices of other cultures, is a great mistake.

Your recent poems deal with social and political events, like Nelson Mandela being released from prison. What do you think about William Carlos Williams's words that it's hard to get the news from poetry but men die every day for lack of what is found there?

One of the strengths of poets is to notice what happens and to tell about it. A man in the audience at one of my readings said, "This is very interesting, but I can't really get into it because I'm a historian." And I said, "Me too." What the poet does, ideally, is talk about the history of the inside of people so that history is more than just the appearance of things.

Do you think that few modern poets write about events outside their own lives?

Poets have to write out of the music that they hear. With minority poets what sounds political is really their lives. When I talk about the black experience in America, I am not talking politics; I'm talking my life. Gwendolen Brooks once said that every time I walk out of my house it's a political decision.

I was at a concert at St. Mary's once, and a wonderful pianist was playing Bach. I love Bach, and, when this man plays, Bach just rises up to the ceiling. Looking around, I started crying. A colleague asked me what was wrong, and I said, " I just wish there were more black people here." He said, "Lucille, do you have to get political?" and I said: "Wait a minute, *you* have the luxury of saying this is political. I'm talking about my life, and I have the right to that."

Do you want to say anything about Audre Lorde's death?

That was a great loss. Every brave spirit that's no longer walking around in a body diminishes the energy. That's some courage gone from the world, some strength, some truth telling, some female power. She's an underrated poet, I think.

You've seen the effects of racism and suffering, as well as richness, in the black community all your life. What are your sources of hope, and what keeps you going?

I wish I knew. I've been asked that before. Some people have been annoyed with me because I'm not bitter. See, I never expected life to be absolutely wonderful. Why would I have? But I do believe in possibility. And I, of course, have to believe that things and people can change. If I didn't believe that, why would I be writing at all?

What sounds like religious faith may just be faith in life, in the human spirit and in human possibilities. Why I have that, I have no idea. Maybe because I have survived, so I know survival is possible. Maybe it's the poet in me. Where she came from, I don't know.

(1994)

Lucha Corpi

Novelist and poet Lucha Corpi was born in Jalipan, Veracruz, Mexico, in 1945. She married as a young woman and at age nineteen immigrated with her husband to California, where she was educated and where she currently resides. Most of her work is written in Spanish and then translated into English. Her best-known works of poetry include *Palabras de mediodia: Noon Words* (1980) and *Fireflight: Three Latin American Poets* (1976). Corpi was the winner of Palabra nueva literary contest in 1983 for her short story "Los cristos del alma" ("The Martyrs of the Soul"). She also received the 1992 PEN Oakland Josephine Miles Award and the 1992 Multicultural Publishers Exchange Award. Her novels include *Delia's Song* (1988) and *Eulogy for a Brown Angel* (1997).

Your poetry is sensual.

Yes, it is full of color, light, flavor, and a multiplicity of things that attract the senses.

Your poetry isn't descriptive; it's based on images. Do you generally use a central image?

I like classical music, and sometimes I write with background music. For example, I wrote "November 2nd in June" while listening to "Scheherazade." Somehow the piece became part of my poem. In "Chess" a spider gives a certain balance to the poem. I had been working on it for three nights, and at last I saw a little spider going up and down; it was precisely the element I needed. (The poem concerns a king who asks the spider to grant the virtues of Mercury.) In "Black Romance" the flavor of vanilla seeped into the poem because, while I was writing, someone was baking a cake, and the odor of vanilla filtered through the open window. When you're in the creative process, a certain vulnerability emerges, and you open to all possibilities. Our lives are at skin's surface, and it feels like we're walking in the open air.

Your poetry has a musical quality.

Yes. I engage with poetry musically. I think I hear the music of the poem before I put words to it. The poem comes to me as if it were a song more than a string of words or images. If I can't transport that musical quality to the poem, then the poem doesn't exist for me. If I don't hear it here, inside, it is not anywhere at all. Part of the process occurs because I studied music. I have been playing the piano since I was eight, and my father liked music from all over the world. As a girl, I listened to Argentine tangos, Spanish music, flamenco, *jotas* [popular Spanish dance]. My musical education was extensive: I studied folk and classical at the same time. Several of my poems have musical titles: "Two-voice Sonata," "Prelude," "Fugue." "Fugue" started as a musical poem. In fact, it became a poem about my life because a fugue is similar to an escape and the beginning of a new course. It's how I faced what my life became after I left Mexico.

Sometimes your poetry reminds me of Emily Dickinson's poems; I'm sure you're fond of her work.

Of course! I discovered her as an adult, but I'm fascinated by her poems. I think that my poetry is an intimate personal experience, like Dickinson's.

I like the short poem very much, although, as I kept on writing, my poems lengthened. Suddenly, one feels that there's much to say, that one needs to expand over many pages. But I realized that even my long poems are made up of shorter ones. For me the image of the poem is like a cell that joins another.

Is there something specifically feminine about your poetry?

Domestic poems, like "Scrap Labor" or "Vegetable Protocol," speak of my reality. My house is my laboratory, set apart from the rest of the world, and when my son was small I spent most of my time there. I often wrote poems while doing housework. I always had pencils and paper throughout the house: in the laundry, in the dining room, in the kitchen. While I do housework my mind is free to write. When something comes to mind, I run to jot it down and then continue with my work.

Lucha, what memories do you have of your childhood?

I am from Jaltipán, a town in tropical Mexico. It's small, with some two thousand people, and, although I lived there until I was eight, I have few memories of it. Frequently, adults tell you things you did, and you feel immersed in a flood of images that you doubt because you don't know whether they're really yours or have been reconstructed for you. When I began to write about my childhood, I tested my experiences to see if they were my own or if I had learned them through the testimony of my family.

From the time I was seven I have a more vivid sense of what happened. I remember rain on the roof: true tropical storms with lightning and thunder that lasted all night long. Everything is excessive at the edge of the tropics. In that environment a person feels a part of nature; sounds of the leaves provoke a state of alert, and there is a subconscious intent to identify each noise. Even today, when something moves among fallen leaves or the wind moves them in a particular way, I turn to see if it is a snake.

In "Nocturnal Solarium" you describe San Luis Potosí as very cold, with a stone soul, and saturated with religious resonances.

Yes. We moved there when I was nine because my father was offered a better job in the telegraph office. San Luis was not as pretty as the tropics. Central Mexico is a hard place to live. The climate is temperate in San Luis, but it is cold and dry in winter. Until I was nine I had never worn a coat, only a light jacket. Language was another problem; the regional accent was Spanish, and I frequently suffered the mockery of the San Luis people, who found my speech was amusing. The patios of the houses were closed, and the windows were protected with bars. It was like moving to another country; it was a tremendous cultural shock.

How are these changes reflected in your poetry?

For the first time in my life I could not express what I thought without being punished. The society was conservative, religious, and acutely class conscious. I could never speak in favor of the fieldworkers or the poor. Country people had to work so hard, and sometimes, because of heavy rain or lack of water, their corn crops were ruined. In spite of that, the fieldworkers went to church the first of each month to give their tithe. This is the Catholic Church of centuries ago. I started to see the contradictions between the priests driving their late-model cars and the poor getting poorer every year. My spiritual conflict started then, and it still exists. Although my ethics have continued to be Christian, I never returned to the church.

In your poetry you speak of the "peasant who poked the earth," and there are references to the exploitation of the farmworker. But at an early age these themes must have been forbidden to you.

Of course! One of the poems in "Solarium" tells of a water boy, Tirso, who taught me to curse and how they washed my mouth with soap to teach me not to repeat what he taught me. As an adult, it was not soap that they used but repression, punishment.

I wrote "Solarium" when I returned to my town in Veracruz. Then I started separating my own memories from those of others, and that is the reason it looks like a search into the past. I tried to picture it more or less chronologically.

The image of the grandmother appears in "Solarium," linked with silence. Although she does not speak to you, one can detect a complicity between you and her. After you have been repressed, your grandmother appears again, looking at you serenely from a distance.

Yes. For the first time, when writing the poem, I realized that there were many things in common between my grandmother and me. My paternal grandmother cared for her two sons all by herself, because my grandfather left her when the boys were small. I divorced when my son was barely two and a half years old, and I also had to bring him up by myself. My grandmother was the first to make me understand that my marriage was a consequence of the way that women are socialized. She was a strong, wise woman who died at ninety-two. Her success came from focusing on the positive part of life.

You left Mexico in 1964 and headed for California. Your poem "Mexico" evokes the country that you left long ago: "Sometimes I think of you / in afternoons like this / an old illness returns." Is this a nostalgic estrangement?

Living in California, I can tend toward one culture or the other, but in reality I have neither. I had never confronted the fact that I had left Mexico and that I could not return. My collection *Variations on a Storm* starts with a long poem entitled "Margins," in which, twenty-five years after leaving Mexico, I confront that uprooting.

I went to a meeting of "border writers" in El Paso: five or six poets, Chicano writers, a couple of short story writers, and some sixty Mexican writers. There I realized that for the Mexican I am too Chicana and for the Chicano I am too Mexican. For the "gringo" I don't even exist! It is a tremendous existential problem, because the question that comes up after all that is: "Where am I?" This happened while I was writing the poem "Margins," and I started to think about the reasons for my not having returned to Mexico. Living with a small son, divorced, in a Catholic country, in a society as conservative as San Luis Potosí, meant having to be the daughter of the family again, and I was already a mother. I was twenty-four, and I could not go back to that situation; it was a matter of self-respect. It was at that time also that I wrote "Mexico."

My exile is not what one would ordinarily consider political, but it is really, because it has to do with the condition of women. I stayed in the United States, although I did not want to accept it completely. And now, as I say in a little poem, "I live with my stomach here, and with my heart on the other side of the river."

This internal division is common in Chicana literature.

I have just written an essay for the Poetry Center of San Francisco about Chicana literature, and one of the things I say is that there was no Chicana literature before 1848, when the United States took the Southwest, which is the Northwest of Mexico. After that date, and during the next hundred years, literature was frequently written in Spanish, until Chicanos started moving to the cities. The literature changed when Chicanos, educated in English in the city schools, began to express themselves in English rather than in Spanish. I think that Chicano literature will take a long time to become part of the literature of this country, because of the confluence of the two cultures.

What do you see as the predominant tendency in Chicano literature, one that tries to integrate with the Anglo world or the one that deals with the traditions and myths of Mexican culture?

Chicano literature tries to reinvent myths and cover them with something, but that is not an isolated phenomenon; something similar is happening in all literatures. But what is different is that the term *Chicano* is being replaced by *Hispanic*. A while ago I went to Chicago to talk to a group of secondary students. The term *Chicano* does not agree with them. The word *Chicano* has a clear political content. It has to do with the 1960s in Berkeley, with the

Third World strike that consolidated the blacks, Asians, and Indo-Americans. The term *Chicano,* that is to say Mexican American, means people of color, people of Mexican culture, and it includes the Mexican Indian and the Pre-Columbian cultures. Its objective is the search for power, the voice and vote, within American culture. The term *Hispanic* only refers to white Europeans and leaves aside our culture, our history, our cultural heritage that makes us different from the Spaniard.

In the series "Marina" you offer an innovative perspective on the historic character of La Malinche.

There are several theories about who Malincin was and what happened when Hernán Cortés and the other Spaniards found her. *Malinchista* means traitor; it used to be the worst insult that one could use against anyone. I never understood quite why, and I asked myself what reasons she might have had to commit an act of treason. A woman did not have any kind of power then. Even in our own times it's difficult to own one's life; one can imagine what it was like then. In my last year of school I did a project on Chicano literature. There was scant material available about the Mexican Americans but less still about the Chicana. I discovered several books about Malinche and devoted some time to studying her. I read those books with a different perspective from when I was a child, because by that time I was already divorced and the mother of a little son. In Mexico, until not too long ago, a woman did not have rights over her children, and the father could take them any time he pleased. In most cases the fathers didn't want to assume responsibility for the children, but the law favored them if they changed their minds.

The figure of Marina touched me deeply; the poems about that theme were the first serious ones I wrote. When I studied Marina I stopped seeing her as a historical figure, and I approached her as a woman whose son has been taken from her by the conqueror, Hernán Cortés. When her son returns, she feels repudiated by him because she is an Indian. Her presence was a mirror for his mestizo nature, something that the young man wanted to forget. He wanted to be Spanish like his father, the victorious colonizer. This is Mexico's conflict since the Conquest. The Mexican hates his father for treating his mother badly, but he wants to belong to that paternal world.

Malinche is usually presented as a woman attracted by the white conquistador.

She was attracted by power; she wanted to be on the side of the conqueror and not on that of the vanquished. But I wasn't interested in writing about this. Many people have done it, even calling her a prostitute. For me Malinche has a tragic stature, because she was a victim. Why did she want power? Because she had never had it; she wasn't the owner of her own life, and her people had sold her. To me she's the first woman in the history of Mexico who decided about her own life.

Another poem, "Black Romance," has resonances of Lorca. In it you present a woman, Guadalupe, subjected, raped, and with a cursed fate that ends in suicide: "From the branch an orange hangs / still without the promise of a bloom."

Close to four hundred years and the development of a country lie between Marina and Guadalupe, but Guadalupe is almost the same as Marina and also a poor Indian woman who has been raped. The poem is related to the sad history of one of my students. In reality her life did not end in suicide, but it had ended nonetheless. One day she told me: "I am living dead; I walk and do everything, but my soul is not here." What is more terrible is that the rapist gave a goat to the girl's father (in the poem the object of trade is a fine mare) as restitution for her stained honor, and the father accepted it to maintain the social order. It's an arrangement among men. The honor of the woman is the property of the man. The mother's role is superfluous; in the poem she throws some salt over her daughter's shoulder to keep away the evil spirits. But nobody is interested in what happens to Guadalupe; nobody worries about her.

My student's story moved me very much. In the poem that identification surfaces because both my spirit and my heart were involved. I believe that the poetic act is a process of involvement.

Even intellectual poets must believe in the marriage between the poet and the image. Six months after I wrote "Black Romance," I read it at a gathering, and several women approached me to ask if that had happened to me. Interestingly, when I showed the poem to my student, she didn't recognize herself in it. Then I realized that the poetic process is interpretive: it comes out of one's own experience and is different from reality.

There is a certain melancholy in some of your work, like "Brotherhood of Bums."

That is a poem of deep solitude and melancholy. At first I thought melancholy was a negative feeling: I saw it as an enemy. Then I realized that it could be creative. At times I'm conscious that a melancholy moment is approaching. It's as if something—time, perhaps—were suspended. I know that something serious is coming, and I prepare myself and the people around me for it. Melancholia allowed me to plumb the depths inside me. For two years I experienced a poetic silence. Something terrible settled in my stomach and perforated it. I got an ulcer. When it finally passed, my poetry had gained by that silence.

(1991)

Rita Dove

Rita Dove, poet and novelist, has won numerous awards and honors, and her work is included in many poetry anthologies. Born in Akron, Ohio, in 1952, Dove was the first African-American woman and the youngest poet to be chosen Poet Laureate to the Library of Congress (1993–94). Her book *Thomas and Beulah,* which won the Pulitzer Prize in 1986, chronicles the lives of Dove's grandparents, who moved from the rural South to Akron. Other well-known works are *The Yellow House on the Corner* (1980), *Grace Notes* (1989), and *Mother Love* (1995). Dove has become a public personality. She has appeared on *Sesame Street,* Garrison Keillor's *A Prairie Home Companion,* and NBC's *Today Show,* and has been heard on National Public Radio programs *Talk of the Nation* and *Fresh Air.* Dove also wrote the text for composer Alvin Singleton's *Umoja,* which was performed at the opening festivities of the 1996 Summer Olympic Games.

At forty-one, Rita Dove was the youngest writer to be appointed poet laureate by the Library of Congress. She succeeded Mona Van Duyn in the yearlong position; among the women who have held the earlier title, consultant in poetry, are Louise Bogan, Elizabeth Bishop, Josephine Jacobsen, Maxine Kumin, and Gwendolyn Brooks.

"Up until now," says Dove, "I could safely say that one of my predominant preoccupations is the theme of the ordinary individual, the unknown individual, caught up in history. Not in the sense of Napoléon's aide-de-camp, but people like Thomas and Beulah, who live their lives against the flux of larger history. So, in that book we get a clear picture of their lives, whereas all those events that are happening around them, like world wars and depressions, we only see filtered through their everyday lives.

"I'm very interested in getting inside a person's head, with all of those intricate thoughts; then that person can never be lumped into a stereotype again," says Dove.

In her novel *Through the Ivory Gate* Dove struggles to present both her characters and their situation in a manner that would elude stereotyping. On one level the book is a portrait of the artist as a young black woman trying "to create artistic space for herself to grow in." But, when the protagonist, Virginia, gets a job teaching puppetry to fourth-graders in her old hometown, memories of long-ago family scenes surface, and she is left with the mystery of why her family suddenly left town and why her mother is so hostile toward her father's sister. At the heart of the novel lies Aunt Carrie's secret: the consensual incest between a teenaged boy and his older sister.

"What was important to me was not to have people recoil in horror and say, 'Oh this is awful'; I did not want to play upon the standard and acceptable reactions to it but to look at it in terms of the two individuals and how it happened," the author explains. "And then to have Virginia discover that actually she wasn't as shocked as she 'should be,' that she could see how it came about and that it wasn't an ugly and horrible thing. I didn't want easy judgments to be made."

The setting for her first novel is Dove's hometown of Akron, Ohio. Dove says: "I've been writing all my life. When I was a child I wrote for fun. We weren't allowed to watch a lot of television, so reading and writing were my chief pleasures—reading first, of course, and always." She remembers childhood summers spent writing radio plays with her brother, who is two years older. "My father hooked up a microphone you could play through the radio, so we would stand in the kitchen and make up these plays, and they'd have to listen to them, poor souls." In addition to the radio plays and writing books together, the pair also started a neighborhood newspaper. Her older brother was the editor and Dove the reporter until she quit to start her own magazine, called *Poet's Delight.*

"It wasn't until college that I really started up in earnest, revising things and wanting a poem or a story to be understood and felt by someone else." Dove majored in English at Miami University in Ohio. "My parents wanted me to be a lawyer, and I really hated anything to do with law, so this was my subterfuge; English was perfectly acceptable as pre-law. I was taking creative writing courses and loving every minute. When I was a junior in college I decided at Thanksgiving to tell them that I wanted to be a writer— a poet, in fact—rather than a lawyer. And to their credit—both my parents' credit—they didn't really get upset. They took a deep breath, but they didn't blink."

After graduating summa cum laude in 1973, Dove spent a year as a Fulbright fellow at the University of Tübingen in Germany, translating German poetry and studying modern European literature. She then enrolled in the University of Iowa's Writer's Workshop and received her M.F.A. degree in 1977.

"When I graduated from Iowa, I remember feeling that postgraduate kind of panic: I was suddenly cutting loose on my own, and every poem seemed to have the shadow of graduate school over it. So I wrote prose; that's when I began to write short stories in earnest, with a feeling of relief and intense excitement because, though it was a different genre, it had similarities to poetry."

In 1979 Dove married German novelist Fred Viebahn. While he taught at Oberlin College, she established herself as a writer. "I look back on those years of genteel poverty as idyllic. We had a lot of time." She had time not only for music lessons, but also, in those two years, Dove wrote most of the poems in her first book, *The Yellow House on the Corner.* Some of the short stories she wrote during this period, such as "Aunt Carrie" in *Fifth Sunday,* later became scenes in her first novel.

"But what was important about that time was that I got into the habit of writing, of making my own schedule and sticking to it. I think that has come in handy, because you have to be disciplined as a writer if you have a young child. It certainly helps to have a partner who is understanding—and, in my case, who's going through the same thing. But it's still a juggling act. So I'm just grateful that my self-discipline was nailed down during those years right after graduate school."

Although she had already published one poetry book and completed her second collection, *Museum,* before Aviva's birth, Dove says, "I remember right after my daughter was born, in 1983, I was already working on the poems for *Thomas and Beulah,* and I was so panicked that the pit of parenthood was going to suck me under and I was never going to write again. And then I thought, I'm not going to let it happen."

Having received a Guggenheim Fellowship to work on *Thomas and Beulah,* Dove was on leave from her teaching position at Arizona State University the year Aviva was born. Dove and her husband set up an elaborate schedule, with the two of them alternating care of their daughter in four-hour shifts from 8 A.M. to 8 P.M.

"Obviously, I couldn't have done that if my husband hadn't been a freelance writer and had a flexible schedule; it was an enormous help. And then I went back to teaching. What happened then is, I think, the story of many women who all have three full-time jobs: you teach, you do parenting, and you try to write, too. I just was tired all the time. I remember days when I came back home and fell asleep over dessert."

Despite the difficulties, Dove says of motherhood, "As they say, I wouldn't trade it for anything. For all of the time that is lost to writing, I feel that there's a window that I've gained, a window back into my own childhood. It's a constant amazement to me. I find myself being torn, pushed and pulled, between frustration and elation—on the day I think I'll be free to write, school is called off because of snow—but, on the same day, Aviva and I have a great talk, or she discovers something that changes the world for both of us. It's a real roller-coaster.

"In terms of writing, I know that there are certain things that I would not have been able to imagine had I not had Aviva—if I didn't have her now." While she might have tried to write about it, Dove says, "I could not have imagined, really, what it is like to be pregnant, to bear that responsibility. After she was born, for the first time in my life I felt completely vulnerable to the world. I mean, we all feel vulnerable at certain times, but with a child there is this feeling that you would do anything to save her or protect her. And that makes you a hostage to reality, so to speak.

"Sometimes the emotion is fear: my God, I hope nothing happens to her. Sometimes it's just an enormous feeling of vulnerability, having to be open. I don't think I could have imagined what that was like. I see it in my friends who don't have children or who have not been responsible for a child: they can be the most compassionate and caring people in the world, but they don't have that odd fragility that parents do."

Of her poem "Weathering Out," in *Thomas and Beulah,* Dove says: "There's a description in there of how Beulah feels when she's pregnant—she feels that she's floating because she can't see her feet. That's taken from my experience, something I think I wouldn't have come up with had I not gone through that." Beulah's nightmares about misplacing or dropping the baby are the subject of another poem, "Motherhood." And in the middle section of *Grace Notes* there are seven poems dealing with Aviva as a young child, up to the age of three.

Dove is currently working on a cycle of poems, many of them set in modern times, which explore the ancient Greek story of Demeter and Persephone. "The Persephone and Demeter poems are trying to look at mothers and daughters without just dismissing the terms of the myth but really talking about what it's like to lose a daughter, to have her abducted.

What is it like to wait and not know where she is? And what is it like to have her come back?

"I began writing these poems as a response to Rilke's *Sonnets to Orpheus*. Why don't we have sonnets to a female deity? I thought." Dove began writing the sonnets, she says, "without thinking of the deeper implications of the goddesses I happened to choose. I have to admit I was very dense for a long time."

In fact, it was her daughter who pointed out the connection to the poet's personal life after reading a book of Greek myths at school. "She read the myth again and said, 'Oh, yeah, that's like you and me.' "

Dove tries to set aside three or four hours, three times a week, for writing, but her schedule is constantly changing in response to both Aviva's needs and the demands of academe. As a consequence, it's much harder to pick up the thread and keep going, she says.

Dove keeps a notebook handy for the times when a line or a word comes to her, unbidden, but says: "If I were to wait for it to hit me out of the blue, I think I would have written a lot fewer poems. Very often, I will go into my room thinking, I have nothing to say, I'm tired, I really don't want to do this, and then something strikes me. So I'm a firm believer in going in there, sitting down, and seeing what happens. When I began writing the Persephone and Demeter poems, I wrote nine in about eleven days—and then didn't write anything for two months, of course, because I was exhausted somewhere inside.

"When I'm writing poetry, I work in fragments: I don't sit down and write a poem or even a stanza from beginning to end. I'm usually juggling quite a few poems in various states of undress; I work on them almost simultaneously."

Whenever she can set aside four or five hours for several days in a row, she can usually finish several poems at a time. "The system works well for my lifestyle, this grabbing a little time here and a little time there. But it does depend on having enough time to get it all together."

"It can take me an hour or two before I really get started. I find that no matter how much time I allot myself in my study, it's in the last hour that the real writing happens—and I don't seem to be able to trick myself in order to speed things up."

"It's always difficult to stop writing when the time is up. I feel like I'm coming out of another country, like stepping out of the wardrobe in *The Lion, the Witch and the Wardrobe,* saying, 'Oh my gosh, here's real life again,' and not being in synch. I can never write in the mornings of the days that I teach because I would not be able to be articulate and purposeful."

(1993)

Joy Harjo

Joy Harjo, who is a member of the Creek (Muscogee) Nation, was born in Tulsa, Oklahoma, in 1951. Harjo's work, which is often autobiographical, reflects her Native American heritage and depicts the landscapes of her Southwestern home. Her best-known works include *She Had Some Horses* (1983), *Secrets from the Center of the World* (1989), and *The Woman Who Fell from the Sky* (1994). One of her most recent books is an anthology of Native North American women's writing entitled *Reinventing the Enemy's Language*. Before she started to write at the age of twenty-two, Harjo danced with a Native American dance troupe and studied art. She is an accomplished saxophone player and currently performs her music and poetry with her band, Joy Harjo & Poetic Justice. She is also a tenured professor at the University of New Mexico.

You have said that you are an "enrolled member" of the Creek tribe. Can you explain what that means?

It has to do with the controversy among Indian people regarding who is Indian and who is not. This issue has come out because of dealing with the government. The cultural definition of "Indian" is based on who the tribal members recognize as such. This classification doesn't always coincide with that of the federal government, because tribes have different criteria. With the rise of Indians' new age, many people claim to be Native Americans, even though they may only have one great-great Native American grandparent. Nowadays, many academics and writers who by blood are only an eighth or a sixteenth Indian call themselves "Indian writers." They don't connect with their people, except for a name on a piece of paper.

My father is Creek, and my mother is Cherokee, although she is not an enrolled member, because her grandmother refused to sign any white man's papers. (She was a rebel, raised by full bloods in Oklahoma.) My mother is of a mixed Cherokee, French, and English background. She acts very Cherokee but also very European!

You try to reconcile such polarities, and I think you develop this concept quite clearly in "She Had Some Horses."

Yes, the poem says: "She had some horses she loved / she had some horses she hated / they were the same horses." Yes, my poetry is a way to bring together the paradoxes in the world. You are a poet when you understand paradoxes. At first I thought that there was no way to reconcile polarities. For instance, initially, I thought of myself as being either totally white or totally Indian and knew of no way to bring together these forces. The paradox was in my own blood, in my own body. It was difficult to decide for one or the other because I loved and hated both parts of myself. As a poet, I learned to bring all this despairing history together. For me poetry is a bridge over the sea of paradoxes; the sea is the blood, and it becomes a way to join them. It has a value and a promise.

In your poetry you express a sense of the connectedness of all things.

A common belief to all tribal people is that the world is alive; absolutely everything is connected. It's what Leslie Marmon Silko talks about in *Ceremony,* about the world being fragile, about Thought Woman spinning a web of life and creating everyone. Eight years ago I had a dream in which I saw the web of life. Someone was teaching me, and I was taken to a point outside the speed of the Earth, where I saw an incredible web of pulsating life. You could watch how absolutely everyone was together, how what one person said, thought, or did affected the web immediately. There were direct connections between the people in Spain and the people in Oklahoma. Time was not separated by minutes or hours: by thinking of someone, you could be with them immediately. So, in that way time mattered not at all. Given what I understand about life, yes, I believe that everything is connected.

The moon is a central image in your work. To me it evokes the circle in which everything is contained and every part is equally important.

The moon represents ceremony as well as the memory of Earth. We count time by looking at the moon; it represents cycle.

In Indian culture life and death are seen as a continuum, parts of a cycle.

Yes. I don't think that we appear suddenly in the world from nowhere and then disappear. Things don't occur that way in the natural world. I know that there is a world of spirits, of being after. I have been there, although I cannot prove it scientifically.

In Indian culture the supernatural world is an essential part. Toni Morrison once told me that, for her, the supernatural was "another form of knowing." Would you agree?

Yes. The supernatural world is ingrained in our culture, and it *is* another way of knowing. I like how Morrison incorporates that world—which runs parallel to the factual one—and weaves it in and out. *Beloved* does represent the "real" world. In European culture the world is supposed to have three dimensions, and it's constructed in a way that only the five senses can maneuver. There are probably more than five senses; there are probably ten, twelve, a hundred senses, which we haven't developed.

The mythical world is alive and rich. I learn from that world as much as from this one. I have had many visions that tell me more about what it means to be alive on this planet than any book I can think of.

I remember my dreams since childhood, and I have been in many places in them. An important dream, now that I have been to Spain, is one in which a Spanish man came to visit me. He said he had been waiting to see me for a long time. And I realized that he was part of myself. He showed me the history of the conquistadors and the Indian people.

Over the images of blood and destruction was an incredible light, which was the huge power of the sun coming through. It was illuminating a terrible reality, yet it was setting it to rest, and the underlying concept was forgiveness. I don't quite know how to express it—maybe one of these days I'll paint it or do it in music—but it was like a white painting, almost like a hologram of images, that he showed me. It was centuries deep, and yet it was all contained in one time and space, and I was part of it.

The ceremony of the Green Corn dance is about forgiveness. Does it have anything to do with the underlying theme in your dream?

I'm sure it does. The Green Corn becomes a very powerful symbol, an image that resonates in the present. Every time that it takes place, it carries the power of all the ancestors.

It's a cleansing ceremony.

Yes, it is. Forgiveness is part of renewal. It represents the renewal of people, and at that time you are to forgive those who need to be forgiven.

Do you incorporate the mythical world into your everyday life?

I think myths incorporate me into their everyday life. A reciprocal process also happens, perhaps because I am a poet or a woman. I always wear the mythical world around or inside and feel things directly out of it.

Do you see your poetry as having a healing power in the tradition of Indian chanting?

I think some of it does. One of the poems in *In Mad Love and War* is a poem to heal a sore throat; another is a transformation that tries to bring people into love, and another is to do away with fear. "Eagle Poem" is a prayer. I see them as alive forms of dynamic energy.

You play the saxophone. Does music play a role in your poetic perception of life?

I was always doing music, even as a poet; often the poems would come to me first by sound. Certainly, images are important, and sometimes I think I write like a painter. But sound is equally important; sound like music comes to me, with rhythm. Someone said to me—even before I played the saxophone—that my poetry sounded like the saxophone because of the pauses. I don't think that music and poetry are that separate. The origin of poetry is really songs.

It is my understanding that Indian music was primarily functional, that is to say, used for some purpose—for instance, to call the rain. Does it continue to be like that?

Yes. What you make is for some kind of use. This could be eating soup or bringing rain, and both are important. I see my work in the same tradition. I wrote a poem to help my daughter when she turned thirteen. It's very much a part of that. As a poet, I don't want to separate myself from the world but to include myself.

Silko, in Ceremony, *says that one of the worst evils that can happen to a people is to forget one's own traditions, one's own culture. Would you agree with this?*

Yes, because it is what we are made of. The stories create us, and we create ourselves with stories—stories that our parents tell us, that our grandparents tell us, or that our great-grandparents told us, stories that reverberate through the web.

Did you grow up listening to stories told by your relatives?

My relatives died very young. My father died when he was in his fifties, so I am aware of this leak. However, I was taught in my dreams, and my aunt told me lots of stories.

What is your view on maintaining Indian traditions? Silko indicates that traditional ceremonies must adapt to modern times to have value.

Any culture is a living thing, which adapts and grows. What remains static dies. It's most important to have a voice in changes and adapt them so they become regenerative rather than destructive. It's like pruning a tree or a bush. If you prune it too much you kill it, but if you do it right it grows twice as full. It becomes a ceremony.

Can you talk about the role of memory? In Native American literature memory is usually presented as a nurturing force.

Memory for me becomes a big word; it's like saying "world." Memory is the nucleus of every cell; it's what runs life; it's the gravity of the Earth. In a way it's like the stories themselves, the origin of the stories, and the continuance of all the stories. It's this great pool, this mythic pool of knowledge and history that we live inside.

Do you think that the younger generations, for instance, your granddaughter, will be able to continue this tradition of story- telling and preserve the value of memory?

I think so. It's part of her, and it is up to me to convey how important it is to her, to them. That's been the role of grandmothers.

In your poems you talk about a sense of loss, of displacement. How do Indian cultures deal with this sense of loss?

In my work I interweave elements of the past, present, and future. I claim the past, as do Silko and Morrison. I am not talking about data. Morrison, for instance, gave more sense of the history of

African-American people with her novel *Beloved* then any history book could do, because her book is both human and terrible. It's terrifying to enter what I call the psychic wound of the Americas, because it's filled up with loss. But you have to claim the past. It's filled with stories that move you and, at the same time, horrify you.

Indian writers—Louise Erdrich, Leslie Silko, and yourself—talk about the consequences of that loss, such as alcoholism and violence. Will the Native American people be able to overcome this situation?

Alcoholism is an epidemic in native people. I was criticized for bringing it up, because some people want to present a certain image of themselves. But, again, part of the process of healing is to address evil. The very process of the healing is talking about it and recognizing it. Alcoholism is hiding; it comes out of an inability to speak. It's like Tayo in *Ceremony;* not until he has been with Betonie is he able to talk. One has to find the place for his own voice, and Tayo finds that place in Betonie's ceremony.

Let's talk about racism. It seems to me that what lies at the very core of racism is fear—fear of losing power, fear that your culture is under threat—and that fear makes you ultimately destroy the "other." Would you agree?

Yes, I think that fear is the cause of racism: fear of oneself. You don't try to control another group by deviant means—and racism is a deviant means—unless you are afraid of yourself, unless you feel insecure about your own power. When I talk to groups of young Indians, I tell them that it is important to remember that they are not less worthy; it's the racist. So, I tell them that the next time they are treated as a lesser people, they must turn it back. I don't mean act racist but in their mind say, "This is your weakness, not mine." And this is the hardest thing to remember, because you tend to take it in, and it makes you feel shameful.

I'm light skinned, and I have not been subjected to as much racism as my sisters or other relatives, but still I have not been served in restaurants. It is absurd to treat anyone else as less than a human being because you belong to a different culture or race.

It may be impossible for people to transcend differences, but I don't think so. I think there is common human ground. There was a time in my tribe when people were treated according to how they were as human beings. That was what your value was based on, not your skin. It was how you treated other human beings, how you treated the relatives. Nowadays there is something wrong in the world; leadership is not based on love of the people but on how much power or money one has. It is an insane world. Silko deals with this so well in *Almanac of the Dead*. The way the Western world is going is terrifying.

Your poetry is metaphysical, but it is also concerned with social issues. You feel that you have a responsibility toward what is happening in the world.

I don't think that a poet can separate herself or himself from the world. We are charged with being truthtellers of the times. This is true for any poet in any culture. I have done other kinds of writing, but poetry demands the truth, and you cannot separate the poem from your political reality. It's a continuum.

Laughter is also present in your works. "We are in the belly of a laughing god," you say in one poem.

Indian people have a highly developed sense of humor. The writing tends to be much more heavy and intense, and the laughter becomes a release. Indian people laugh constantly when they get together—a teasing, joking, self-deprecating humor that's central to the culture.

In the middle of all the tension and destruction there is a laughter of absolute sanity that might sound like insanity. Maybe laughter is the voice of sense. I always tell my students that you cannot take everything too seriously because it will kill you. If you carry bitterness and hatred around, it gives you arthritis, rheumatism, cancer. Certainly, I have to be aware of everything, but I can't let it kill me.

(1994)

Josephine Jacobsen

Josephine Jacobsen was born in Canada in 1908 and had her first poem published at age ten. In 1995, when she was eighty-eight, her book *In the Crevice of Time: New and Collected Poems* (1995) was nominated for the National Book Award. The following year, *What Goes without Saying: Collected Short Stories* was published. Jacobsen has written several books of poetry, novels, short stories, essays, and literary criticism. She received critical praise for *Let Each Man Remember* (1940). Her subsequent volumes of poetry include *The Human Climate: New Poems* (1953), *The Animal Inside* (1966), *The Shade Seller: New and Selected Poems* (1974), and *The Chinese Insomniacs* (1981). She served as Consultant in Poetry to the Library of Congress from 1971 to 1973 and since 1973 has held the title of Honorary Consultant in American Letters. Jacobsen also was a member of the Literature Panel for the National Endowment for the Arts from 1980 to 1984.

You once told a fascinating story about Japanese artists who, after they became famous, changed their names and started fresh. Where is this from?

A book by Matisse called *Jazz*. He writes that an artist should never be a prisoner of a style, of reputation, or of success. He describes Japanese artists who, in an earlier age, had become oppressed by the accumulation of responsibility, the fear of self-repetition, the terrible weight of expectancy. They wanted, like snakes, to shed their skins and start fresh. So they moved to a new identity, stripped of everthing except a paintbrush in order to protect their freedom. J'aime ça, because I came to this profession so late and in such a curious way, and as it closes in around me, I feel its tremendous weight. I get an enormous amount of requests for jacket comments, for recommendations—all the peripheral part that is so important. When young poets are starting, they desperately need this kind of help. I have never been able to withhold it, and it doesn't seem proper to do so. When you try to separate the profession from the poems, it's like Mae West peeling a grape. When you try to get the grape from the peelings, you realize the profession of poetry has overgrown you like ivy. You have an overwhelming desire to go somewhere and wake up in the morning with a completely different identity.

Your stories and poems deal with the "instant of knowing," sudden self-discovery, terror in the commonplace. Is your world like that?

Yes, life is absolutely brimming with terror. I can't conceive how you can live in the world today and not be aware of it—particularly anyone who feels passionately. A line I wrote at an early age speaks of "the tissue paper between the foot and the plunge." I think we live from minute to minute, from hour to hour, with our friends, our loves, our lives at risk. We are hostages to fortune.

Like that wonderful line you found years ago on a tombstone in a New Hampshire cemetery.

"It is a fearful thing to love / what death can touch."

How do you feel about daring, taking artistic risks?

That's a difficult question, because my daring has been a kind of reverse daring. All of us who are not young have moved through various poetic climates. There have been many periods when the stream flowed toward certain types of poetry—political, social consciousness, structurally innovative—which I approved of and thought absolutely necessary but which were not what I felt I could or should do at the moment. It's just as hard to swim against the stream of the current as it is to be innovative in the technical sense. What I have tried to do is develop my poetry naturally and not be coerced by any topical trend. That is as daring as I have wanted to be.

What are the changes that you see in your work through the years?

I think that there have been manifest differences in terms of technique—approaching and retreating from conventional forms, continually investigating what should be done in and out of specific forms. If you cut into a tree, you can tell its age and check its growth by the number of rings. I would hope that, if my books were compared, the work would show a steady development in depth, perception, and control.

I gather that in recent years you have received many accolades, and demand for your work has increased.

Yes, the picture has changed a great deal. I have work in seven current and future anthologies. Two books will be out in the fall of 1986: *Adios Mr. Moxley,* my second collection of stories, and *The Sisters,* a chapbook. Three critical estimates of my work will come out next year. I have published a great deal, but I haven't had much written on my work. This is a whole new phase.

Do you feel that it is overdue?

All my friends tell me it is. William Meredith made the most wonderful remark a few years ago. He said, "Josephine, you hear a lot about people who are precocious, but all I can say about you is that you are postcocious." This cheered me up to no end. I came into poetry in such a strange way—no academic or professional connections, no input of any kind. I just dropped my poems in the mailbox.

So recognition came late. How did it happen?

I don't understand how it happened. I kept writing, and just after I was married [she and Eric celebrated their fiftieth anniversary in 1982] I sent some poems to *Poetry* (which I later learned got about 60,000 poems a year when Harriet Monroe was editor), and she took some of them. This absolutely stunned me. Then for a long time I was very busy—poetry was the peripheral part of my life. The first thing that made me feel that I was a professional was the success of *The Testament of Samuel Beckett,* which William Mueller and I wrote. I was fascinated with Beckett, who was practically unknown at the time. I felt that sections of his work were pure poetry. In 1971, to my surprise, the Library of Congress called and asked me to be the poetry consultant. [Jacobsen was the first woman chosen since Elizabeth Bishop, who served from 1949 to 1950.] While I was at the Library, Doubleday took *The Shade-Seller.* It was nominated for the National Book Award. I was in my sixties, so to say I came late to the game is putting it mildly.

I gather that, although you had almost no formal education—less than four years in all—your mother encouraged you to read extensively.

I didn't go to school, and either there were no truant officers in those days, or they never caught up with us. Mother had great intellectual curiosity and the greatest disregard for schools. She was very restless. After father died, when I was five, we traveled constantly. I never stayed long enough to develop any friends, but I was not conscious of any deprivation. I read a tremendous amount.

What poets influenced your work?

The three poets who influenced me most at the formative stage were Auden, Yeats, and Archie Ammons. Yeats and Auden influenced me directly into the stream of poetry, and Ammons influenced my whole conception of what poetry could mean to a person.

What did you learn from Auden and Yeats? They are so very different.

They couldn't be more opposite. From Auden I got wit and humor, contemporary language, and that ordinary objects play a part in poetry. From Yeats I learned not to be afraid of grandeur: that myth and tradition and a word that is so dubious that I hardly dare use it—romance—were still part of poetry.

An evaluation of your work in the Hollins Critic *quotes you as thinking of poetry as a "solitary and dangerous encounter."*

I do. I don't know whether my own poetry has been so solitary because I had no connections with any movements or whether it is a temperamental thing. My poetry is very slow in the writing, very personal, though, oddly enough it has never been personally centered. I've never written what is known as confessional poetry.

What do you mean by dangerous?

I think you take enormous risks in poetry. So much poetry is contrived according to demand, is aimed at certain kinds of publications, or is done to enhance an individual reputation. For me it's like Jacob wrestling with the angel. In every encounter with a poem there is a possibility of an abysmal failure. It's like the difficulty of trying to climb a mountain: The chances that you are going to fall are very steep, and the sense of triumph if you get there is very strong.

You have a natural gift for elegant language or style, but your work shows an even greater concern for total creative process.

I have always been baffled by having been praised so often for style, yet I never thought of it consciously apart from the work. I am much more interested in other elements, so that whatever style I developed came out of the work rather than being imposed on it.

Have you ever experimented with different styles?

I started conservatively with lyric and rhymed poetry and then wrote nothing in the way of rhymed poetry for the next twenty to thirty years. A few years ago I went through a period of immense contraction—the desire for compression—and wrote a great many short poems, poems with a very impounded vocabulary. "The Monosyllable" and "Finally" from *The Chinese Insomniacs* are good examples.

Of late you have also become a critically acclaimed short story writer.

I love short stories. I always felt the form was for me. I think the training in poetry, the fact that every single word has a vital importance, carries over into fiction. Most of my poems are poems of movement, of action. Something is happening within the poem, which is a minute story. I admire descriptive poetry, but I write almost none. My primary interest is always people and situations that affect people.

Do you have a particular method of writing?

It is unbelievable how little time I spend writing. Almost all of it has been done in two months a year. For a long time I tried to hew out an hour here or there, but I found it destructive to my work. It's like a pool: If you keep chucking stones in it, you can't get any reflection. I know people who can sit down and write at the kitchen table. Alas, I have to have protective leisure. I can't start unless I know that nothing is going to interrupt until I finish.

How do you feel about past discrimination and its effect on women poets?

I feel very strongly. The first lecture I gave at the Library of Congress, "From Anne to Marianne," dealt with that issue. Nobody in their senses can regard as a coincidence that in the last twenty-five years there were an extraordinary number of excellent women poets, whereas from Ann Bradstreet to Elinor Wylie and Edna St. Vincent Millay there was hardly a women in the history of America who wrote any kind of good poetry. Emily Dickinson was the outstanding exception. Women haven't changed that much. Life hasn't changed that much. What has happened is because of the assumptions that women had no intellectual capacity and that there was nowhere for them to go if they had. God knows how many silent poets went to the grave because being a poet was not a practical, emotional, or mental option.

You talked about Edna St. Vincent Millay's refusal to be pigeonholed.

She was really the original feminist. Emotionally, she had the guts and spirit to relate person to person, not woman to man. She wrote some of the most beautiful love sonnets in the English language.

What about the accusation that most women are emotional, confessional poets like Anne Sexton and Sylvia Plath?

I think both Sexton and Plath were good enough to overcome the element and write some very fine poetry. I don't feel that the circumstantially personal in their poetry helped. I'm not sure that it is a strictly feminine trait. I think it is true that men and women react slightly differently emotionally. Some of my more militant feminist friends would say that is a sexist remark, but I see it as a difference in emphasis, not as an advantage or disadvantage. Louise Bogan and Elizabeth Bishop have a scope and control that many fine men poets lack. And, if you want to get into highly emotional poetry, Theodore Roethke and John Berryman are as emotional as any woman.

Are women as creative artists affected by not having had real power?

Isn't that true of any group that has been oppressed? It's nonsense to pretend otherwise: It's a statistical fact. Being oppressed in America, whether it's black people or women, inevitably breeds a lack of self-confidence, an ambivalence about success.

What is your estimation of contemporary poetry?

What's the Dickens quote, "It is the best of times, it is the worst of times." There is more good poetry—I am not speaking of great poetry, which, alas we don't have a great deal of, but good sound poetry that not only merits reading but has real caliber—being written than in any other period in my lifetime. On the other hand, there is unquestionably more total trash being turned out than at any other time. After four years on the NEA Literature Panel and two years of judging national contests in which there were hundreds of submissions, I probably have as good a grasp of what is being done in contemporary poetry as anyone. I don't think any good poet is going to be threatened by a flood of terrible poetry. So I say let the flowers bloom, let all the flowers bloom.

Do you think that the pluralistic concerns of society are having an effect?

I think there are a great many things feeding into contemporary poetry that it has never had to cope with before. There were so many common assumptions seventy-five years ago that have shattered now. All of us, including me, God knows, are confused about contradictory political and ethical issues in which no matter what you do you come out wrong. The more troubled a society you get, the more poetry you are going to get—good and bad.

What is the role of a poet?

I think that you have to consider the individual gift. I don't approve of the Ivory Tower approach. I like to see poets embroiled in life, involved as human beings, even if it isn't what activates your poetry. The danger is that society pushes poets into situations where they feel they are a separate, excluded group who have to stand off and make statements. Poets are very conscious that they are not writers whom the average person reads, understands, or identifies with. Very literate people who are up on history, biography, and novels haven't read a poem since "Hiawatha."

What is the next step in your work?

In what I'm doing now the scope has widened and there is something from my whole life that goes into each poem. The poems have got to be deeper and wider. The recent poems are more concerned with universal things that are also highly personal— themes like life, death, love, honor, loneliness, betrayal—experiences that condition everyone's life. There is always the risk that once you leave the personal, you get into rhetoric, and if there is no universal root, you get personal statements with no wider application. I would hope that I will continue to examine each poem in light of that. I wrote a poem called "The Sea Fog," about the fog coming around this vessel and all the doors and stairs being changed and finally coming down to the stateroom in total isolation looking in the mirror and saying: "Who are you? Do you really have any idea who you are?"

When you say "Who are you?" who should one be?

Again I come up strongly for differences. For me it would be integrity, speaking of what you really have learned, what you really know, not what someone wants to hear or what you think is going to advance your worth or what is going to be most remembered. I think that, when poetry or religion or patriotism or art is manipulated for personal gain, it's the bottom line, or, as my kids say, the pits.

In a lecture, "One Poet's Poetry," you said: "The essence of poetry is the unique view—the unguessed relationship, suddenly manifest. Poetry's eye is always aslant, oblique." What do you mean by oblique?

Poetic vision doesn't see things head on. The poet's angle of perception is not like any other. Emily Dickinson said it best: "Tell all the truth but tell it slant."

(1986)

June Jordan

June Jordan is one the most anthologized living poets. She was born in New York City in 1936 and is currently a professor at University of California–Berkeley. She is also an essayist, playwright, biographer, children's author, and political activist. Jordan has written over twenty books. Her recent book, *Kissing God Goodbye: New Poems 1991–1996,* includes a collection of political essays as well as poetry. She is also a lyricist—she wrote the libretto for the opera *I Was Looking at the Ceiling and Then I Saw the Sky* (1995), which has been performed across the United States and throughout Europe. In addition, Jordan has co-starred in a film with Angela Davis, talked architecture with Buckminster Fuller, and had coffee with Malcolm X.

Your parents came from Jamaica, and you were born in New York. Tell me a bit about that.

My father actually went from Jamaica to Panama and then here. When my mother came, she had to borrow shoes for the journey. She was from an indigent village that I finally saw when I became an adult. At that time it still didn't have full electricity and running water. She left, obviously, for a better chance. I think she had finished high school. She worked here as a domestic to help put her younger sister through high school and college. Then she became a nurse. My father came from a large half-Chinese, half-white family even more destitute than my mother's. He never finished grade school. He went to Panama because they were using a lot of Asians to dig the Panama Canal. He came to this country when he was about nineteen years old. After teaching himself how to read, he became a post office worker. My parents' efforts secured them a working-class sort of security.

I would say that they harbored rather typical immigrant expectations. The differences, if any, were that they were more impoverished in background than the parents of most people I know. They moved to Harlem separately, which is where they met. My father became, among other things, very active at the Harlem YMCA, which was a political kind of place at that time.

What years are you talking about?

The early 1930s, I guess. My father got involved in the Marcus Garvey Black Nationalists and in teaching other young black men how to box. He had a schizophrenic attitude about his identity. Sometimes he was into Black Nationalism; other times he was adamant that he was not black at all. That meant a lot of conflict for me.

I surprised my parents because by the time I was two I was reading very very well. My father took me for a series of intelligence tests, and I was designated a little genius. My father, who had just taught himself how to read, adopted a dictatorial program of forced instruction for me. From the time I was two he crammed me with stuff to read, to recite, to play on the piano, to sing. My mother's expectations, on the other hand, were different. She belonged to a chapterless black church specific to Harlem. Her vision was that I would be a help to my people, meaning black people. My mother was very clear about who she was, a black woman. My father, belonging to a High Episcopalian Church, was just about Catholic. It was in that church that I was confirmed. He made all the decisions about what was going to happen with me—going to camp, to prep school, and so forth. My mother endured the whole thing. In fact, she was completely uninterested in my report cards, whereas my father questioned an A minus.

Growing up with these parents, I probably acquired predictable expectations of this country. I thought if I worked really hard and shined my shoes, everything would go well. West Indians put enormous emphasis on education. We never had a car or anything like that. That was never even in the picture. The idea was school.

I grew up in Harlem until I was about six, when we relocated to Bedford, which was rapidly becoming black because the white people had fled to Brooklyn. We moved from Harlem, which was a kind of community, because it was public housing, to a neighborhood where there were two kinds of housing. One was little homes that people could buy, which is what my parents were doing, with little backyards.

The Bedford community was a completely all-black universe. I think, in a way, that has had a lot of influence on me. It wasn't until I was sent away to school, where I became the only black person in this other kind of universe, that I was really aware of white people at all or even thought of myself as black particularly. I just thought of people as good people / not good people, nice / not nice, cute / not cute, and so forth. Not until I was taken out of that community did I became aware that I represented something. As a matter of fact, when I was going away to prep school for the first time, my mother said to me, "You are representing the race." That is a ridiculous burden for kids. A lot of people my age at that time had that burden put on them by their parents. It was not a question about accepting it or not. I tried to be a good girl.

How did you live the 1960s? And what basic changes did you see for yourself and for the black community?

I think that was the first time that a consciousness of a national community emerged. You met people from all over who had to deal with the same kinds of life-threatening things you had to deal with because you are black. That was a revelation. There was the simultaneous revelation that you could *do* something: wage a revolutionary effort to make your life more equal, if not fully equal, here in the United States. That was true for white as well as black.

I also began to think about this country as problematic. Until then I was coasting along on whatever my parents had instilled in me about what it meant to be an American. Suddenly I didn't think of myself as an American; I thought of myself as a black American. All these precepts and things are written down in the founding papers, and to find out that you were never even under consideration, that you are three-fifths of a person at best, is pretty shocking. Then I saw all the white violence against us as we tried to secure equal rights. That was startling and radicalizing for me.

I tried to participate in the nonviolent part of the movement, but I discovered that I am not nonviolent. I have to do something now. If you hit me, I am going to go for you. I had problems with what was happening in the South under Dr. King's leadership at that time. Subsequently, I've grown up a bit. Then, I couldn't believe it. It just sounded outrageous to me, and wrong. To ask us and to ask children to submit nonviolently to assault and insult just violated me.

There was a connected action, combatively connected.

It was a huge mass movement nationwide; otherwise, the changes never would have happened. It was not just a movement; it was a huge disruption of business as usual. The other thing was that people participating in all of these demonstrations were risking their lives, and that is pretty serious. When people are willing to do that, you know you've got to deal with them. They are not going to quit, to forget it and say, "Never mind, I don't really want to vote."

They are saying: "You are going to have to kill me to get me to submit to the status quo here. It is not acceptable." Indeed, many people died. It was huge; it was disruptive and actual. You say it was nonviolent, but I realized subsequently it wasn't really nonviolent. It was deliberately provocative. In other words, you could have had a huge nonviolent demonstration, but if you didn't have a response of white violence, there is no story. That was the idea: have your enemy respond. In a way it is nonviolent, but the revolution really depended upon the provocation of horrendous on-camera white violence. But white people really came through: again and again and again.

You have written twenty-two books. What compels you to write? Is it to help human souls, to help people lead better lives?

You have to split it up because poetry is one thing and the novels and the political writing another. Some of my poetry is political for sure. In any genre I try to change things. For the sake of freedom based on justice and equality for everybody. That is my purpose and the way I fight. I love to fight! I used to duke it out; now I use words. I write to create something beautiful, something different, something to be remembered. To share with other people.

How have you been received as a gifted American poet?

It has been difficult for me, because I am a female poet as well. I have two things going against me. To get comparative I would say not well enough yet. That is changing. My friend Adrienne Rich is upset that I don't have more recognition and critical attention. Her book on poetry and politics, *What Is Found There,* speaks about me, in fact. She wants to do an interview that will put me on the map.

Many things I have done as a poet are technically new. I haven't gotten that kind of craft recognition. People don't understand what I am doing, just technically speaking. I know the craft of poetry thoroughly, like very few other people alive today. So when I make choices, it is a knowledgeable process—which takes somebody like Adrienne Rich to be able to recognize. She, of course, knows her craft inside out. Many critics treat my work almost entirely on a sociological basis. When it comes to a dissident black poet, there is very little spontaneous inclination to check out that person on a technical level. It is heartbreaking a lot of the time. On the other hand, I began as a black poet, trying to serve my community as I defined it, which was black people. I don't define myself like that anymore. I just say I am a poet or an American poet. This is my country, and everybody in it is my people. Increasingly, I am putting myself at the disposal of many different kinds of people.

From the outside it seems African Americans are working and writing for African Americans, Chicanos for Chicanos, Native Americans for Native Americans.

I don't think the "hyphenated" identity of different peoples in the United States is going to disappear. What may happen is that more people are going to become hyphenated in the way they understand themselves and the way they present themselves to other people. For example, no longer will the people of color be the ones who hyphenate themselves. Irish Americans, Italian Americans, German Americans, and other peoples who until now have designated themselves as whites (which is stupid—what does that mean?) will have to get into the particulars of their cultural and racial history. Among other excellent developments will be that the historical meaning and residence of the term *white* will necessarily be blown away. White is right: that is all it meant. Might and right. There is going to be a lot more intelligence, among other things, in the intercultural, interracial, interethnic dialogue.

You say that schools are political institutions that teach power to the powerful and something destructive to the weak. Can you comment on this?

Well, that has been the case traditionally for sure. If you just look quickly at the history of education, at least in England and here in the United States, for the longest time the only people who could learn how to read and write were males from families of property and wealth. That was to maintain the power of the powerful. If you notice, powerful people do not have a problem about education.

The guys running the multinational corporations are the interna-tionalists; they make it their business to find out, or find somebody who can find out, about Chinese culture or whatever. If they don't have that knowledge, they can't deal. When we get down to regular people, this suddenly gets to be the big debate.

You have read books by African Americans, white men . . .

White men essayists, white men novelists, white men poets, all writing about themselves. Then we had other white men writing about these guys. There is a message that goes along with this: if you are not one of those people, your status in the curriculum is optional—an *elective* we call it. Your life is optional; it is not manda-tory. It is not imperative that you or anybody else knows about your history or your traditions, the literature you've produced. It is not imperative. It is imperative that you know about Homer and Socrates and T. S. Eliot.

If you don't know yourself, you are up for grabs. Anybody can tell you anything, and you'll accept it. If you are growing up in a dominant culture that views you as despicable or inherently inept and you don't have any knowledge of yourself, you are going to have to buy that. On the other hand, if the dominant culture is saying there is something inherently wonderful and superior about being a man or being white, if you don't know that your Swedish ancestors came to this country because they ran into ruin and fam-ine, you believe you were always running the country. You have white people who really think that nothing in their history had to do with the struggle for survival. It leads them to be really hostile toward people who talk about that.

They don't want to acknowledge that.

Most people in the world had a tough time. If you look at the way most people present the United States, you would never know that. You would think the only people who have trouble are people of color, some kinds of crazy women, and gays and lesbians. We are optional types. Everybody should get real about who they are and where they come from. Then there would be a solid personal basis, not a rhetorical one, in which we can make connections. What did it take to get you into this great big house? How many ancestors had to die to bring you to this place?

I agree with you; you have to know your history first to be able to know others. After the 1960s I think it is a second step.

The civil rights revelation led a lot of people, including myself, to a separatist period. When I became a stone black nationalist, I wouldn't talk to anybody. The women's movement has also gone through separatist periods, and there are separatists in the gay and lesbian movement now. Apparently, this is something that people have to do. If you study other people's histories, just inside this country alone, you know what a separatist period is going to produce. It is a dead end, and it never leads to anything good. Just like nationalism of any kind never leads you to anyplace good. A lot of people in this country are so ignorant, they don't know that the Nazis were a nationalist movement. Everything nationalist eventually takes you to Auschwitz. The people running the camps may change color or language, but it is still Auschwitz.

As a teacher, what readings do you give to your students?

I use what I guess you would call a cross-cultural syllabus. So, if the theme is coming of age then I'll try and have Maksim Gorky's *My Childhood,* James Baldwin's *Go Tell It on the Mountain,* Sandra Cisneros's *House on Mango Street,* Amy Tan's books. Then we just get into every single one of them and try to find connections or important differences. I try to get the students talking and writing about themselves in that context of coming of age then see within the community constituted by that class if there are any important commonalities or really important differences. One of the new courses I am doing is called "Poetry for the People," representing as many different kinds of people as possible. I hope to attract all kinds of students who will want to test themselves as poets and then present them to as wide an audience as we possibly can. The other course is called "Coming into the World Female." I am going to use a cross-everything approach on that one, too.

What happens with language at school, English, if you have an audience in which you have Chicanos, blacks, and so forth?

Particularly in the poetry classes, but also to some extent those classes that require students to write in prose, I try to help students to develop their voices. That has to mean accurately differentiating use of language. I try to tell them that if you are really using English well, it should be possible for somebody to guess how old you are, what part of the country you come from, and what your class background, sex, ethnicity, or race is. That, of course, is an ideal of sorts. I think that gets them going. If you read something and you don't have a clue, it probably means it is not good writing. It is just like the way they put things in the *New York Times* or academia—who knows who wrote it. That is the idea, I think, of standard English. God's English. We have imposed upon us in this country one language, English, despite many languages. There is a way of speaking that is considered normal, which is white, male, middle-class, East Coast. Tom Brokaw, the guy on television—that is the way you are supposed to talk. That is normal. That is patently absurd.

Obviously, that is a lot of power if you can say the only language that will be used, will be spoken or written here, will be my language. Not too long from now most people in this country will not have English as their native language. What I encourage my students to do is to write in a bilingual way whenever possible. Sometimes when they give poetry readings they won't read in English; they will read whatever they have to say in whatever language it is. If you don't know it, that is just too bad. When I was growing up in New York, a lot of people came from Puerto Rico. Everybody talked to these kids in English. It was unbelievable: these teachers had no bilingual capacity whatsoever. Then they would test the kids, who didn't have a clue what the question was, let alone the subject, because it was all in English. So they were all being trapped into these remedial crushes. This is very serious politics. It is unbelievable. Look at countries like Nicaragua, and you see that this is not necessary. The best poets in Ireland, Wales, and Scotland write in two languages all the time. At least 50 percent of the time when they give a reading in England they read in their language.

What is your perspective of language when you write poetry?

I write essays to put together an argument, basically. I know what I think about Bosnia. The question is, how am I going to write in a way that constitutes an argument that might persuade somebody who doesn't agree with me at the start? So, it is a persuasive function. Language has to serve in a practical sense in my essays.

Poetry is about telling the truth, for me, anyway. That is how I teach my students. You have to undertake to tell the truth. That necessarily demands extreme attention to accuracy and precision. All those things leads to concision, which, in turn, yields intensity. All I have to do is tell the truth: I didn't feel this, I didn't feel that. I guess I have a quasi-religious attitude toward language in general. That comes from my early upbringing in the Christian church. The word itself is bold, sacred.

(1994)

Janice Mirikitani

Janice Mirikitani, who is a third-generation Japanese American, is a poet, editor, choreographer, and social activist. She was born in Stockton, California in 1942. Some of her best-known books include *We the Dangerous* (1995), *Shedding Silence* (1987), and *Awake in the River* (1978). In 1970 Mirikitani cofounded *Aion*, the first Asian-American literary journal, and in 1980 she edited the first bilingual anthology, *Ayumi: A Japanese American Anthology*. Mirikitani is also one of the founding members of Third World Communications, a coalition of third world writers, artists, musicians, and poets. A longtime community activist, Mirikitani has won several awards for her community work and is currently the Executive Director of Programs of Glide Church in San Francisco—a position that she has held since 1969.

How did your family come here?

My grandparents immigrated from Japan through Hawaii in the early 1900s. Like many immigrants at that time, they worked on a plantation—until they saved enough to come to California. They could not buy land because they were immigrants. But my mother and her siblings were born in America, so they could purchase a small farm. My mother is a nisei [second generation of Japanese immigrants], and she married my father by "bichampany," or arranged marriage. They divorced around 1946, after we were released from the concentration camps.

My whole family was incarcerated in lower Arkansas, in addition to 120,000 other Japanese-American citizens relocated to concentration camps throughout the country. I was an infant and have no memory of that time. After the war, when we left the camp, my grandparents returned to the farm, which the government had confiscated. Of course, my grandparents had to rebuild. It was a tremendous loss. My parents moved to Chicago because of the anti-Japanese feeling on the West Coast. My mother was a single parent who worked two or three jobs to survive. She remarried several years after she divorced, and we returned to the farm. It was not a happy childhood with my stepparents: We were very isolated.

In California?

Yes, in the small town of Polamo, north of San Francisco. My mother and stepfather raised chickens, and we built our own home and developed the farm for about ten years. After I graduated from high school, we moved to Los Angeles. I graduated from UCLA, got my secondary teaching credential from UC-Berkeley, and taught school for two years. Then I returned to San Francisco State to get my master's degree.

This was the late 1960s. I had just decided to take a leave from school to earn some money, and I started to work part-time here at Glide Church. It was an interesting crossroads for me, because I had for many years attempted to be white, middle-class, and accepted. I realized that I was *not* acceptable and that I was not white. It took tremendous crises to get me to that point: the war in Vietnam, the civil rights movement, the ethnic studies strikes, my work here for poor communities and people of color.

I worked with my husband for about fifteen years before we got married; we have been married for eleven years now. As an African American, he was very involved with various situations in the ghettos across America: the riots in Hunter's Point in San Francisco as well as the marches in Selma. He brought that kind of consciousness to this place.

Glide Church is a nontraditional, progressive place to work, and I was encouraged to become involved in my areas of interest. At that time I was intrigued by alternative publishing, because people of color were not being published. That provided us with stimulus and motivation to create our own presses and platforms to make our voices heard. I edited three or four anthologies of people of color, including one called *Ayumi,* which presents four generations of Japanese in America. That became one vehicle for expressing my activism, in addition to organizing artists to protest apartheid and dictators like Somoza and Marcos.

I think that the nexus of capitalism and militarism brought writers and artists of color and of conscience together, to express our views, to let our voices be heard, and to create solidarity. That was a sea change for me, because it forced me to see my own denial about who I was and who I needed to become: an Asian-American woman with a history and a political consciousness. Certainly, my history within the camps was a metaphor for my awakening consciousness of hard ghettoization. Ghettos are like concentration camps: isolated, with little or no access to institutions of opportunity. I see it in my work here. It is a challenging place, one that does not allow for complacency. Poor people always point up the reality of what is happening in the country and the world, because they feel first the effects of economic, political, and social injustice as well as racism and classism. Again, I suppose that is why I dedicate myself so much to this place— because it keeps me grounded and forces me to look at the social issues that inspire the work and the writing. (Although I don't get enough time to do the writing!) It also challenges me to do my own healing and to confront issues that force me to grow.

What affects my writing at this point are some of the women's programs I helped create. We don't deal with recovery as an isolated issue. The majority of the clients are African Americans. The drug of choice is crack cocaine, because it is cheap and it is being fed into the community. You don't deal with the chemical only. You have to address the racism, the childhood abuses, the feelings of rejection and worthlessness. We started groups for many different areas of abuse. As part of that, I had to face my own incestuous childhood and to admit my own addictions to powerlessness, self-hate, and self-destructiveness.

I recently returned from reading at an international festival in Wales. Maya Angelou (who was responsible for my being invited) closed the festival with her performance. The Welsh were so receptive and vocal about my presentation. The universality of our pain is is quite striking. But, again, the circle of recovering women constantly forces me to face myself and what I have to do.

Occasionally, I would ask my mother about the camp experience, and she would change the subject. When as an adult I became involved in the movements for Asian Americans, people of color, and ethnic studies, I became obsessed with the camps. But she would not speak of them. Her silence became my metaphor for for our oppression and the attendant self-hatred. And the invisibility that America creates. Rendering you invisible is the worst form of rejection. It says you just don't exist. We are indifferent to you; in fact, we don't even feel enough about you to hate you.

I think of silence as a form of suicide. My mother chose to be silent, yet I know she experienced pain each time she thought of the camp. To articulate words about the experience would cause her to relive it. I understand because a woman from my grandmother's generation took me in her arms and shook me and said: "You don't even begin to understand the pain. She is doing this because she has to survive. She has endured things for you." I believe that is true for any generation of people who have to undergo unspeakable cruelties and humiliations to make sure that you are here, that you have opportunities. My mother was brutally deprived of four years of her life. I also think she was battered. She bore that in silence because she did not want to impose the pain. Perhaps that was simply the way she had to do it.

Silence gives you power. If I choose not to speak, I don't allow you to know how I feel.

I think that is very Asian, too. If you don't speak or show your feelings, you can be mysterious, and no one will truly know you; hence, no one can hurt or control you. I believe that is true for many men. The issue of saving face is very important: You don't disgrace yourself in public. That, of course, is not just Asian men.

A young woman I went to school with spoke only when she had to. I call the story I wrote about her "Martha's Smile" because she would smile all the time. I never saw her sad or mad or teary. Everybody liked her because she was so sweet. She certainly never challenged anybody. I was loud, reckless, rebellious, and all those angry things, because I was an abused kid. I got jealous of her in grammar school because my boyfriend started to flirt with her. I grabbed her hair, threw her to the ground, and pummeled her. She laughed the entire time, while I cried and scratched and screamed.

She jumped off the Golden Gate Bridge at the age of twenty-five. She had been lied to by a married man who told her that he loved her and was going to marry her. My immediate reaction was anger at this man for deceiving her. Then I got angry at her. The man did not murder her. Her silence killed her because she couldn't tell about her hurt.

I write about these things because I think it is healthy to express these thoughts or these feelings of violence and rage in words, so that you don't have to act them out. That is what is saving the lives of the women I work with.

Again, back to the silence of the camps. I absolutely understand it now. My mother did finally break her silence, like many many nisei did, in 1981, when the government made monetary reparations to the Japanese Americans. Many people broke their silence; it was a catharsis for all of us.

You write about women and violence.

As a sexually assaulted person, I do see connections between sex and violence. Women are vulnerable. There is a sickness in society that causes men to feel so powerless that they have to use brute force to dominate. There is a similar dynamic when it comes to war. That America bombed Grenada, of all places, is ridiculous. Vietnam, the same thing. Tons of bombing and napalm over villages that have eight hundred people in them. It is just absurd. It is like dropping a nuclear bomb on a mouse because you have to show your muscle.

I was on an empty plane once with my infant daughter when two soldiers came on. They were obviously serving in the army—it was during the war. They sat in the two seats next to me, so I had to put my daughter on my lap. Being at that time demure and not very vocal, I said nothing. My daughter started to cry, and the man sitting next to me leaned over so close that he was touching my shoulder and said, "Stop her, stop her, stop her crying." Thank God the stewardess came. Well, he wouldn't move. I knew my child was in danger. I didn't know what was going on except that he was in a village somewhere listening to a child cry, and he was going to harm it. I got up. I had to move. So I've seen that hatred; I've felt it; and I'm trying to capture it. I don't know or understand these feelings, but I have had them perpetrated against me.

You also explore the feeling of loss, separation, not belonging to a racial point of view.

It is dangerous for me to generalize, but I've heard other women express a sense of their lives being stolen from them. Like fathers who abandon. You internalize blame, because if you were lovable enough they wouldn't have left you. A sexually abused person realizing that they don't have the physical strength to stop the abuse has lost a core thing. Your power is taken from you. Not only do you not feel loved; you feel gutted. I don't know how else to say it.

You feel strongly about loss.

Yes. Sometimes when I go to a class to do a special presentation, I want the kids to experience the losses the Japanese Americans suffered. I give them an assignment: You have three days to pack only what you can carry and only what you are allowed to take. Your mother says you can take only one item that is precious to you. What would it be?

Let's talk more about racism.

Racism is complicated . . . I think it is a reflection of an unfinished soul. It is also an institutional issue. There is no light at the end of this tunnel. It is ensconced in every institution: schools, publishing, corporations. You rarely see a face of color in a boardroom. In movies or television, Asian people are exotics. They don't speak, they never have leading roles, and they never have a dynamic relationship with a major character. They are the evil ones or the servants. The women—usually sex objects or bar girls—are serene, quiet, and sweet. And you always know that, in a mixed relationship, the person of color is going to get killed. We are expendable.

Your story about the survivors of Hiroshima who came back here is very sad.

It is true. American citizens visiting family in the bombed cities were trapped there during the war. When they returned to their homeland, they were ostracized because they had radiation sickness. Even their own communities did not understand. They couldn't get medical insurance because they didn't understand the causes. One woman could not touch her family because they thought she might be contagious. Can you imagine not embracing your grandchildren?

Something else you deal with—in your story of Doreen, for example—is the standard of beauty in this country.

Each of these characters is myself as well as other women I know. The woman on whom I based Doreen perpetually distorted her face. I knew a Japanese-American woman who dyed her hair blond, and, because dark hair does not take blond dye well, all her hair fell out.

I have gone through this myself; I taped my eyes for about ten years. I used lemon and bleaches and all kinds of things on my skin. I even caught poison oak so my face would peel and lighten up! I went through just incredible torture about my hair. I just wrote a piece last night about the hair. We used to rat it, mound it, back comb it, perm it, and do all this crazy stuff to look like the white girls.

I read that when Japanese immigrants came to California the Japanese community would wait for them at the harbor and take them to have their hair cut Western style.

The Japanese are quite conformist: They don't want to stick out or call attention to themselves. The Chinese keep their customs more, speaking the language, wearing the clothes and the braids.

Many Japanese immigrants were poor farmers who came seeking richer opportunities. Now many Japanese have gone into the "professions." I was determined not to be a farmer's wife. My half-brother is a surgeon in Pensacola. He was always determined to earn a comfortable living, to bring pride to my family—and he succeeded. He is very obviously the favorite because he is my mother's son and my stepfather's only child. I have come to a place of peace with myself about it, although it hurt me very much. Because we were very poor and didn't have refrigeration, my mother said: "Janice, you have to save the milk for your brother. He is the boy. He is younger than you are. He needs it." There were many little things like that. Again, that is not a self-pitying statement; it is an example of how you are a lesser priority. My mother is not cruel; she is a good person. Clearly, her son was her pride and joy; he got the money to go to college, whereas I had to get scholarships.

You are married to an African American. It seems that Asian and Native Americans are concerned with their own. Is this a continuation of the American idea of individuality—that we are different, really?

I think so. I believe that we must be about self-definition. You cannot come to the table as an equal if you are trying to be anything but who you yourself uniquely are. Within the Asian community there are many different ethnic groups, each with their own cultural differences. The ideal is that we attempt collectivity, yet racial and class injustice make it difficult.

Is it difficult to be married to an African American?

The only way that I have stimulation and interest for myself, and for the relationship, is for me to be myself. To make sure that I don't advocate to his power, fame, or culture. I don't try to be African American. I can't: It is not authentic. I struggle hard not to be Mrs. Cecil Williams, the minister's wife. Without my own Asian identity I've lost the deepest part of my core.

It sometimes seems to be difficult for his people to accept me fully, for they have their own stereotypes, and the impulse of a community is to to want you to be with your own. There is a certain self-preservation in that.

White people still call me a cute China doll and ask me house-wifey kinds of questions. They expect me to fulfill a certain role because I am Asian—which is nuts.

African Americans who know Cecil but don't know us as a couple have come to our house for a political event and asked if I was the caterer, florist, housekeeper, chauffeur, or even gardener. I'm sure that Cecil gets it on his end, although my community is not as vocal and is smaller.

We've had to struggle somewhat with our families. My mother and biological father have their own set of stereotypes to over-come. My mother cried when I told her we were getting married, but now she just loves Cecil. But you can't be around my husband and not love him! He is so sweet and good to people. His family has slowly accepted the fact that we have our unique way of being with each other. It is a difficult question, undoubtedly, and I don't like to say things that sound divisive. I believe that, for all of our sakes, we must begin to talk to and hear each other, for our differ-ences as well as for our common ground. My husband says that human beings are more alike than they are unlike, in sorrow and in laughter, and in the things that move and motivate them.

We must be in the world. We must hear the words of the world, including its pain. If we don't do that, we won't survive. Especially as people of color. We won't survive without each other.

(1994)

Alicia Ostriker

Alicia Ostriker, poet and critic, was born in 1937 in New York. She cur-
rently resides in Princeton, New Jersey, and is a professor of English at
Rutgers University. Ostriker has published eight books of poetry, contrib-
uted to many periodicals, and written criticism on the Bible. Her work
has been translated into several languages. Her books include *Stealing
the Language: The Emergence of Women's Poetry in America* (1986) and
The Nakedness of the Fathers: Biblical Visions and Revisions (1994).
Ostriker has won numerous prizes and awards, including a Guggenheim
Foundation Fellowship and grants from the National Endowment for the
Arts and the New Jersey Arts Council. In 1986 her book *The Imaginary
Lover* won the William Carlos Williams prize, and she was recently named
as a finalist for the annual National Book Foundation Award for *The Crack
in Everything.*

Alicia Suskin Ostriker, fifty-five, was one of the first women in America to publish poems about her experience as a mother. She began composing the title poem of the chapbook *Once More Out of Darkness* during her second pregnancy, in 1964–65. "I started writing about motherhood almost as soon as I was a mother. My first long poem about pregnancy and birth was put together from jottings I'd made during my first two pregnancies, which were eighteen months apart. At that time I was writing because writing was what I did. It didn't occur to me that I hadn't seen any poetry about pregnancy and childbirth until I was well along in shaping that poem ["Once More Out of Darkness"]. That was a radicalizing moment for me as a writer. So I started writing from a maternal perspective before getting to the point of feeling imprisoned by motherhood—that came much later."

Ostriker's first child was due in August 1963; in the same week she handed in her Ph.D. dissertation. Six months after her second daughter was born in February 1965, Ostriker began teaching at Rutgers University, where she is a professor of English. Her son, Gabriel, was born in 1970. Three factors influenced Ostriker's decision to combine career and children in an era when few women did: ambition, a desire to organize her life differently from her mother's, and a husband who said he would divorce her if she ever turned into a housewife. Her husband of thirty-four years, Jeremiah P. Ostriker, is a professor of astrophysics at Princeton University; the couple lives in Princeton, New Jersey.

When her children were small, she recalls: "It was pillar to post. I constantly felt guilty for not doing enough for my students, not doing enough for my children, not having time to write, and so on. This is a familiar story: there were never enough minutes in the day, and I was always exhausted. But I was keenly aware and proud that this was my choice. I didn't know anybody else who was trying to have babies and a career simultaneously. I did have the support of my husband, so the exhaustion, the craziness, and guilt were balanced by my strong sense of intentionality. This was a life I was choosing, and I didn't want to give up any piece of it."

Ostriker, who has a B.A. degree from Brandeis and an M.A. degree and Ph.D. degree from the University of Wisconsin, says: "Being a college teacher was something I'd wanted to do for years—that's why I went to graduate school. Writing my dissertation, on the other hand, was complete hell. I swore I would never write another critical book after that one. Later, I changed my mind on that score."

Ostriker's dissertation, "Vision and Verse in William Blake," initiated her career as a Blake scholar. "One reason I worked on Blake, who was my guru and my main man for many years, is that his writing is so revolutionary. He was a protofeminist; he explores the meaning of maternity and paternity in our culture more deeply than any previous poet; and he writes about the experience and the significance of sexuality more interestingly and more powerfully than any poet before D. H. Lawrence."

In the midst of her busy life as professor, wife, and mother, Ostriker continued to write poetry, as she had since childhood. She had neither a specific time nor a particular place set aside for that writing. "Poetry was always in the interstices of everything else, the nooks and crannies. It was always time stolen from other responsibilities. Everything else in my life was being done for someone or something else: someone needed me to do it or I was being paid to do it. Poetry was the one thing that I did for myself alone, with the sense that no one on earth except myself gave a damn whether I did it or not. In my early years I didn't make other things move over very much for it; it was always on the run.

Where did I write? Everywhere. I wrote while I was driving. I wrote sitting on buses. I wrote on the living room sofa. I wrote in bed. I even shared a desk in my husband's office at Princeton. I never did much writing at Rutgers because if you kept a typewriter in an office there it would be stolen.

For many years it was difficult for me to do any concentrated writing at home—not counting jots and scribbles. Scribbling something down in the first place can be done anywhere because it's done spontaneously—it just happens. But the work of revising needs peace and quiet. Concentration was difficult for me at home, because home was the place where I was responsible, where I was the mom, even when someone else was ostensibly taking care of the children. I just necessarily always had an ear to everything that was going on. We had Au Pair girls for ten years, through the time my son was three and we started sending him to daycare. Having an Au Pair helped, but home was still the domestic rather than the writing space."

When the family moved to its current residence, in 1975, Ostriker gained a study, which doubles as a guest room; in the years since her youngest child entered high school, she has been able to do more concentrated writing at home. But even then, with more time and a room of her own, Ostriker's method of writing poetry has not changed. "For me, the initial writing of poetry is never place dependent because it always interrupts something else that I'm doing. I never sit down and decide to write a poem."

Ostriker illustrated the covers of two of her early books of poetry with her own woodcuts. Although she was able to write poetry "on the run," she was not able to continue doing graphic art. "That was the real trade-off," she says. "When I had children, I stopped putting time into art. I had taken courses in graphics and did etchings and woodcuts. That turned into annual Christmas card making with the kids, which was the only kind of sustained visual project I ever did after they were born. I carry sketchbooks and still enjoy drawing, but graphic art requires time and space." She has not gone back to graphic arts, "because the writing meanwhile expanded exponentially."

Her children have been a major theme in all of Ostriker's books after the first. *The Mother/Child Papers* places family life in the context of history. It was begun in 1970, when her son Gabriel was born, a few days after the United States invaded Cambodia and four student protesters were shot by members of the National Guard at Kent State University. The first section of the book includes poems that juxtapose the joy of giving birth with a mother's horror at the violence of war and her fears for her son's future. Ostriker writes:

she has thrown a newspaper to the floor, her television
   is dark, her
intention is to possess this baby, this piece of earth, not
   to surrender a boy to
the ring of killers. They bring him, crying. Her throat
   leaps.

Among her more recent works with a maternal theme are the sequence of poems to her older daughter in *The Imaginary Lover* and a suite of birthday poems to her younger daughter in *Green Age*.

Ostriker speaks in the measured tones of a professor; she is clearly accustomed to having her words copied down in the notebooks of her students. Asked to what extent motherhood influenced her imagery in general, she answers: "My guess is that the experience of maternity saturates every single thing I do. Maternity augments one's vision, one's sense of reality, one's sense of self. I believe that I'm maternally motivated toward the world and not just toward my children. Certainly, I'm maternally motivated toward my students, who are a big part of my life. But in addition my views of art, history, politics, all sorts of issues, are in part determined by that double experience that motherhood brings of idealism and practicality. Children represent at once infinite hope and stony intractability—and the world is like that, too.

I have found that my poems about family and children are often what audiences are most engaged with and most responsive to. When I read the mother-daughter poems from *The Imaginary Lover*, people will always come up from the audience and request copies for mothers or daughters. These are themes that speak universally to audiences and to readers. When I and others first began writing about motherhood, however, the literary and critical response was, of course, this doesn't belong in poetry, this is trivial, it's not universal enough. One change in the literary scene since I started writing is that it has become quite normal rather than exceptional for women to write from the position of motherhood. It was almost unheard of when I started writing, but it doesn't surprise anyone now."

Does that also mean that poems on a maternal theme are accepted now within the academic world and taught in university courses? "That, of course, moves more slowly, just as any avant-garde work exists before it's accepted. Canonization obviously takes longer than production. I would say the most important poets being taught now who write as mothers are Anne Sexton, Sharon Olds, and Maxine Kumin. Maxine is certainly accepted in the canon (she was poetry consultant at the Library of Congress and is a chancellor of the Academy of Poets). A great piece of her work is what she calls 'the tribal poems.' "

Another change Ostriker has seen is in the attitude her women students have toward motherhood. One class in the 1970s had such a negative reaction to the pregnancy/birth theme of her early poem "Once More Out of Darkness" that she wrote "Propaganda Poem: Maybe for Some Young Mamas." Her students today see maternity differently. "There is no longer a feminist party line opposing motherhood. That has fortunately faded away. Young women today, I believe, see motherhood as a personal rather than an ideological choice. What has not changed very much, although it has changed to a certain degree, is the extent to which fathers are prepared to invest their time and souls deeply in the nurturing and raising of their children. I know some couples in which the fathers take equal care, but they are exceptional." In her own case, although her husband has always been very supportive of her work, in terms of helping out with the children, Ostriker describes him as "more supportive theoretically than practically."

Asked what advice she would give to young women on combining creative work with child rearing, Ostriker notes, "The most important thing for a young mother to remember is that children and the experiences of maternity—ranging from ecstasy to hellish depression—are valid material for art. We require artists to explore and define the significance of all human experience, and the vision of motherhood that mothers will propose is obviously going to differ from the views of 'experts' such as male doctors, psychologists, and novelists. Mothers can use their lives as raw material for art just the same as Monet used landscape or Dante used Florentine politics. They can record everything."

"One of my great regrets is that I didn't write down more. You think you'll remember everything, and then you forget." The poet urges women to keep journals and use tape recorders, cameras, and video to capture fleeting moments. "And don't be afraid to be honest," she adds. "Don't sanitize your feelings, don't be sentimental. The culture has plenty of sentimentalized versions of motherhood. What we need is reality—the whole array of realities that have never before gotten into books," including the realities of those who are not white and middle class.

In retrospect, Ostriker says of her own experience in combining writing and mothering: "I'm sure that many people will tell you this: taking care of children is a tremendous drain on your time, your spirit, your feelings, your self-image, and there's no way around that. The positive side is that having children keeps you real, keeps you open and on your toes, and is a continuing learning experience. It gives your mind and your passions a constant workout—which, if you want to keep them alive, is not a bad thing to have happen."

Now that her children are all in their twenties and living away from home, is she still able to give her passions a constant workout? "I worry about that a lot. I worry about cooling down, and I try to find other ways of keeping hot. The question of what to replace motherhood with is a real question when you've defined yourself as a writer for many years through motherhood, as I have. When that consuming and absorbing interest subsides, what can you find to replace it? I think I'm still in the process of discovering that."

(1993)

Linda Pastan

Linda Pastan was born in New York City in 1932. Pastan has won several poetry awards, including the Dylan Thomas Award, the Virginia Faulkner Award, the Alice Fay di Castagnola Award, the Bess Hokin Prize, and the Maurice English Award. Her book *PM/AM: New and Selected Poems* (1982) was nominated for the National Book Award. She has been awarded several grants and was the Poet Laureate of Maryland from 1991 to 1994. Her most recent books are *The Imperfect Paradise* (1988), *Heroes in Disguise: Poems* (1991), *An Early Afterlife: Poems* (1995), and *Carnival Evening: New and Selected Poems, 1968–1998* (1998). Pastan is also the author of the acclaimed *The Five Stages of Grief* (1978).

Poetry is disease. Yet one does not get well by curing the fever.
On the contrary! Its heat purifies and illuminates.
                                       —*Franz Kafka*

"When I finally complete a poem, there is simply nothing more exhilarating." Linda Pastan gazes off toward a ceiling corner and smiles. "There is great joy in being a writer. The discoveries you make about the world and about yourself give the greatest pleasure. The real pain is when I can't write."

Indeed, Pastan herself suffered a painful silence of almost ten years before she began writing again in 1964. "I was married quite young. I got the Master's in Library Science—it's a completely unused degree—because my father agreed to support me for another year if I got some type of professional degree. But I hated it, and I never used it. Instead, I decided to have a baby." Stephen, born in 1956, was followed by Peter in 1957. With her husband, Ira, in medical school, Pastan managed to get a full grant from Brandeis, where she received an M.A. degree in English. When Yale offered Ira a residency, they moved to New Haven, and thoughts of a Ph.D. dissipated, as Yale did not accept part-time students. Pastan exhibits neither bitterness nor remorse; career juggling had never entered her mind nor anyone else's at that time. "You just went where the best place for your husband was available," she states straightforwardly.

Despite the pleasures of family life, Pastan describes the silenced years as unhappy. With her husband's encouragement and support, she began writing again in 1964 and established a daily regimen (which she still maintains) of four hours' work in the morning. "That's the minimum," she adds. In 1965, when she gave birth to Rachel, she "basically already knew what to expect," and managed to juggle writing, childbirth, and child rearing. She had little trouble getting published. "There was that *Mademoiselle* thing when I was in college." (She won the Dylan Thomas Poetry Award in 1955.) "I was looking back at that recently and noticed that the runner-up was Sylvia Plath—which just shows that contests

don't mean much," she shrugs offhandedly. Her nonchalance, how-
ever, is not a front for false modesty. Pastan looks directly at you as
she talks, her gentle eyes exuding a genuine sincerity. She speaks
of herself easily and candidly—initially with a tinge of shyness—
pausing occasionally to scan the ceiling to find the precise lan-
guage to articulate her thoughts.

When Pastan began writing again in the mid-1960s, she pub-
lished in various periodicals. In 1971 she compiled her first book,
A Perfect Circle of Sun. Her sixth and current collection, *A Fraction
of Darkness,* continued her exploration of danger, loss, and death
and of coping and coming to terms with these issues in late
twentieth-century America.

Nestled within several acres of woods, Pastan's house is about
ten miles outside Washington, D.C. Nature has always figured
prominently in her poetry as a metaphor.

"Metaphor is my major interest," she comments. She has al-
ways loved poetry and knew it was her real voice. When she began
writing at ten or eleven, the subject matter of poetry suited her: "I
could write about 'adult' subjects like trees and the sun; my stories
always sounded childish."

When Pastan was about twelve, she became obsessed with
death, even though no one she knew had died. Death continues
to be a major theme, yet she is far from suicidal. Her face dark-
ens, and her eyebrows furrow. "I think suicide is immoral, primar-
ily because the people you leave behind never recover." Poems
such as "On the Death of a Parent" and "Go Gentle" typify her
preoccupation with mortality and with similar concerns of middle
age. The recent loss of her father also figures prominently in her
poetry.

"My father was a very dominant person and a charismatic
surgeon. He wanted me to be a doctor." As a result, there was
much conflict. An only child, she describes her childhood as "not
easy." She winces then squirms uneasily in her desk chair, seek-
ing language that will make her sound neither bitter nor ungrate-
ful. Pastan views herself as a lonely child, one who spent a great
deal of time alone and grew up with books. A contemplative
melancholy—so vivid in her poetry—emanates from her person;

even when she smiles, her kind, basset hound eyes betray a soft sadness lurking within.

Pastan considers herself an outsider, one who, as in "The Winter at 16," thinks of herself in the third person. "I always feel more an observer than a participant in life," she explains. She admits to being melancholy—even gloomy. Although she professes to be "basically lazy," her mind obviously works constantly as she acts, observes, and writes. "There's always a poem going on in my head."

Two basic stages make up Pastan's writing process. First, she sits at the typewriter and "lets it all pour out. Just the raw images, without any craft." Later, as she shapes the poems, she applies her intellect and her learned skills. Once she completes the poems, she sends them to her daughter, now a junior at Harvard, for critiquing. "They come back all marked up. She's got a good eye and is quite a good writer herself," Pastan beams.

"It's that second stage that can be taught, but the first part is either there or not." Pastan admits that she has always had that initial vision; nonetheless, one of her greatest fears is losing it. Helplessly, she casts her palms and her glance outward, signaling her own contingency to Kafkaesque forces. In "Voices" she writes:

> Someone who knows told me
> writers have fifteen years:
> then comes repetition, even madness.
> Like Midas, I guess
> everything we touch turns
> to a poem—
> when the spell is on.
> But think of the poet after that
> touching the trees
> he's always touched,
> but this time nothing happens.
> Picture him rushing from trunk
> to trunk, bruising
> his hands on the rough bark.
> Only five years left.

Although her current collection concludes with a sestina ("Shadows"), and she is working on a set of six sonnets, most of her poetry is free verse. The classic forms are easier for her to write than free verse: "half the work is already done for you. But I think that having something looser fits my subject matter better."

Her forms may have changed slightly over the years, yet all of her poetry consistently has examined the same themes. "It's just the surface that's different." Pastan drifts off a minute and thinks. "I'm aiming for clarity but without simplicity—clarity of image and idea combined with complexity. I know it's not trendy to say this, but I want an accessible surface. I want my poetry to be accessible to all types of readers. If I can't get some sensual or intellectual response from all different kinds of people, then I've failed." Pastan does not want her audience to be limited to literary critics.

Likewise, she does not pigeonhole herself as being a particular type of writer. Despite the Jewish influence evident in her poetry, she does not consider herself to be a writer in the Jewish tradition whose depth could be appreciated only by Jews. "My grandparents were Orthodox, but my parents were firmly atheistic. I never set foot into a temple until I was twenty and went to a wedding. Most of my Judaism is acquired and learned. But I feel very Jewish. The Holocaust has great emotional resonance for me, but we are nonobservant. Of course, I have classic Jewish guilt, and I guess I was a typical Jewish mother—overprotective." (She laughs.)

Being as significant an influence as her heritage, Greek mythology serves both as muse and subject. It is no accident that the poetry Pastan has been writing lately centers around Eve and Penelope; much of it is a continuation of themes she has explored before, most notably in *Aspects of Eve*. She is currently working from three different translations of *The Odyssey*.

Pastan appears little bothered that her work revolves around the same themes. When asked of her attraction for the Midas imagery, she responds that it "came out of my writing about the sun. A number of years ago, an interviewer asked me why I write so much about the moon. I hadn't realized it, but, when I went back and looked, I realized I had. So I made a conscious decision to write about the sun." Looking over her typewriter toward the woods, she chuckles, "But they'll never get the leaves out of my poems."

When the Pastans built their house twelve years ago, they were influenced by a media report regarding the benefits of sunlight. With walls of windows and skylights, "there's really nowhere in the house where there's not a lot of sunlight."

Like Pastan herself, the house is casual, comfortable, and unpretentious. Surveying the woods through ceiling-high windows in her study, Pastan remarks that "one of the reasons I like Washington so much is that I can choose to live in the wilderness, but the city is only half an hour away. Plus, I don't have to dress up all the time"—she shifts and wriggles, as if shedding the pretenses and trappings of political and social Washington—"which I hate."

Pastan's poetry, also shorn of pretense, explores the grander themes of love and loss, light and darkness. Despite her vision of light and of the earth's beauty, she cannot shake her awareness of our own mortality, her knowledge that our lightness on earth is temporary. In her poetry she tries to penetrate these shadows, and these shadows penetrate her work. In the concluding sestina to *A Fraction of Darkness,* she writes: "Always save your pity for the living / who walk the eggshell crust of earth so lightly, in front of them, behind them, only shadows."

(1986)

Minnie Bruce Pratt

Minnie Bruce Pratt was born in Selma, Alabama, in 1946. Pratt has published three books of poetry: *The Sound of One Fork, We Say We Love Each Other,* and *Crime Against Nature,* which won the 1991 Gay/Lesbian Book Award given by the American Library Association. She is also the author of a book of stories, *S/HE,* which was a finalist for the American Library Association Gay, Lesbian, and Bisexual Book Award for Nonfiction. Pratt currently lives in New Jersey and teaches for the Union Institute, an alternative university.

I'd like to begin by asking you about your long narrative poem
Crime against Nature, *a passionate expression of what it's like to be
separated from your children and your past because you are les-
bian. In putting the book together, did you feel that the need to tell
what happened was more important than the poetics of the work?*

It is in fact a long poem, but I didn't think of having to make a
particularly coherent narrative out of it. Putting together the pieces
had more to do with thinking about my readers—how they would
be able to pace themselves through this difficult material—and
wanting to organize it in a way that didn't just focus on myself. The
longer poems in the collection are more expansive and go out
from me to a larger community space. I was concerned that people
reading the book not see it merely as my own personal story but as
in some ways an allegory of what happens to other lesbians and
other women due to oppression.

In Crime Against Nature *there's a poem called "All the Women
Caught in Flaring Light," which is set in a lesbian bar.*

I recently spoke to a predominantly heterosexual audience, most
of whom didn't understand that it was a lesbian bar, which upset
me. In fact, I wrote that poem because, at the time I was writing the
book, I would read at women's cultural spaces and lesbians would
come up and tell me heartrending stories. I felt a responsibility to
tell some of them. I guess it's what happens when you're a writer in
a culture of repressed groups.

*I hear you saying that writing entails a certain degree of responsi-
bility.*

I think the concept of writing or art as just self-expression or self-
fulfillment is a Eurocentric and sterile patriarchal idea.

Sterile in what way?

Because it goes only one way. And it's not a way of conceiving of art
that acknowledges that you are able to make art only because things
come to you from your community. The image of the individualistic,

egocentric artist—white, male, and heterosexual—is premised on him creating all by himself in defiance of his culture. But that's not how I have made *my* art, nor is it how most people in repressed cultures create. You make art only in the matrix of your community, and you're pretty foolish if you don't think that that's true. Responsibility isn't a grim thing, you know, in that context. It's just what's real. You are fed, and you feed.

Feeding and nourishment seem to be two different concepts. You were fed a fairly conservative diet growing up in the South. You mention the influence of the Fugitives on your early writing— people like John Crowe Ransom and Allan Tate. One of your sons is named "Ransom." How did you discover and develop different influences?

That's an interesting question. The Fugitives were a conservative, reactionary set of white, male Southern poets who basically supported segregation and were my cultural models for poets in the modern era. I started reading differently when I began teaching in historically black schools in North Carolina. That was my first exposure to the tradition of subversive and transforming literature. I began to read African-American literature and quickly discovered writers like Toni Morrison and Alice Walker.

In Rebellion *the essay "When the Words Open" describes hearing Audre Lorde read her poetry. She was the first writer and the first poet you heard speak publicly as a lesbian. When you're doing an interview or a public reading, do you imagine that there's a woman out there who might be appreciating what you are saying in the same way that you appreciated Lorde?*

I certainly hope I'm of that kind of use to young lesbian writers coming along! When people come up to me and talk about their work, I have that feeling. When I'm alone and writing, it is very hard to keep believing that what one is doing means anything to anybody in that moment of isolation. I remember the people who say to me, "Your work taught me this" or "Your work has meant so much to me." They're part of a circular process. I keep trying to give it back, either by how I talk to people about my work or in the work itself. The ending of my essay "When the Words Open" has a series of allusions to folks who have said things to me about my work, including a woman who wrote me a letter from prison whom I talk about as being an inspiration.

What are your thoughts about lesbian aesthetics? Is there a particular way of writing that you would consider to be specific to lesbians?

This question keeps coming up. Is there a woman's language or a lesbian language? I would say that there is no one language for any one people, and lesbians are many, many peoples. We are from different cultures; we speak many different languages.

Do you find a problem in using pronouns?

It's not the pronouns but, in a larger sense, how to avoid lesbian merging in your writing. We all have to grapple with the *she/she* and *her/her* pronoun dilemma (or strength), the doubleness of femaleness in lesbian writing. That's the literal linguistic element of the problem, but the larger question is, how do you differentiate between the two women, and how do you show the boundaries? How do you give all the particular areas of the togetherness and separateness that exist between lesbians?

I suppose you're familiar with the controversy we have had in Canada over appropriation of voice, whether, for example, a non-Native writer should be telling Native stories. What's your feeling about this?

I find it problematic to deal with writing in someone else's voice because I was raised in the segregated Deep South, which fed me lies about people who were different from me. I feel that those lies contaminated my imagination. I heard a tremendous amount of irrational material about difference that I have had to spend my whole life unlearning. If you're going to write about someone different, you have to be able to trust your imagination to take you to that person. I'm not saying it can't be done, but I find it problematic because I'm so aware of how deeply my unconscious has been contaminated from infancy.

What will you focus on in the address you are going to give at the conference here in Toronto?

One of the things I'm going to talk about is the challenge of teaching a class as an open lesbian teacher and why it's important to deal directly with lesbian issues, whether or not one does that as an open lesbian teacher. It's important not to just shove lesbian issues to one side but to deal with them head on in the classroom, especially if one is teaching women's studies. The controversy right now is over a woman teacher bringing lesbian issues into the classroom. In another era you couldn't be a married woman and teach. It really is about what's acceptable to do as a woman occupying a position in an educational system that's supposed to be a replication of heterosexuality. Before you even start talking about what *books* you're going to use, you have to be ready to address that root premise.

Just because you have the materials doesn't mean that you're going to challenge the structure. Actually, I think the most effective way to deal with not just lesbian and gay studies, but women's studies also, is to have lesbian, gay, and feminist material across the curriculum while maintaining the separate programs or departments as autonomous spaces.

This leads me to a related topic—the National Endowment for the Arts. Your erotic poem "Peach," from your second book of poetry, We Say We Love Each Other, *was read before a committee of the NEA when they were accusing you of obscenity. Would you like to say something about this experience?*

Chrystos, Audre Lorde, and I all received an NEA grant, and Senator Helms got upset simply because we are openly lesbian. We were on his list, along with many others, as examples of the misuse of federal money. Helms asked the general accounting office to investigate whether money was being misused. Eventually, they didn't pursue it, but it was the beginning of a long period of feeling discouraged and traumatized. It seemed like any day I might open the *Washington Post* and discover that my work was being used in nasty ways on the floor of the Senate. It was educational because I thought I was out in about every possible way, and I realized I was not out to the Senate! I wasn't sure how I was going to deal with that. Well, I never had to go before them, but the NEA turned down a number of grants to other gay, lesbian, and feminist artists.

We held a big demonstration at NEA headquarters. People disrupted the proceedings, including a former student who shouted out my poem "Peach" at the height of the whole thing. I didn't hear it, but I imagined it, which was quite wonderful.

Since then the NEA controversy has been revived by arch-conservative Patrick Buchanan. He was campaigning in Georgia with a videotape consisting of excerpts from "Tongues Untied," Marlon Riggs's wonderful film about black gay men. Buchanan pulled portions from the film and made a tape denouncing the NEA and its misuse of federal money. He is running it saying, "This has nothing to do with racism or homophobia," and so at the same time generating those messages. Here's an exceptional piece of work by a gay artist being used illegally, against all copyright laws, to turn people against us.

We put our work out there, then it's seized on by the reactionaries, dubbed obscene and pornographic, and used against us. That's why it's so important when folks say my work has helped them as lesbians, as gay men, as heterosexual women. I'm really conscious of others out there who want to take my work and use it in negative ways.

How long were you unable to write after this harassment?

Not for about six months. It tapped into a very early self, probably preverbal, preconscious—the child who was raised in the authoritarian, segregationist South and who was told, "Don't think, don't talk." If you start thinking and feeling too much about the Other and the Different One, you won't be able to stand what you're doing to them.

I'm interested in your exploration of religious traditions. Although you are highly critical of Christian demagoguery, you write with intense feeling about Jewish customs and rituals in which you have participated.

Ritual in my growing up years was mainly associated with Catholicism, and Catholics were to be feared because they used rituals and images in their worship. In "The Maps of My Bible," the last essay in *Rebellion,* I write about going to Seders with my lover. I take participation in the rituals of other people very seriously; it's not something that I do often or on my own. I go to her ritual space only by invitation. Most of my experience with ritual has been informal, woman centered, and woman invented—Wiccan, circles, and other kinds of rituals. The rituals I take part in now are mostly my own.

Do these involve writing?

Well, there are certain things I do before I write. I have a writing altar and a relationship altar. My main writing altar has a picture of Barbara Deming that my lover, Joan Biren, took and postcards people have sent me with women from different cultures, including Ella Fitzgerald in a red suit and hat (looking fabulous) and a Ghanan woman cooking in an iron pot in her traditional robes. I keep that one because I think of the African-American women boiling clothes in iron pots behind my great-aunts' house when I was growing up. I have a bluebird's egg and shells from the Cahaba River where I grew up and a little cedar box filled with Chinese fortunes (I don't save the bad ones, so if I'm feeling discouraged I pull out a fortune).

Your work seems to be immersed in a consciousness and feeling for land, of place. There's a deep spiritual and sensual quality to it. Is this a result of being brought up in the South?

I think it's related to ruralness, although the sense of the South as a separate place—for African-American, white, and Native American folks—is intense. I have on my altar a jar of dried clay chunks from one of the country roads to Selma from my house. I suppose that if I were to denote any base for my spirituality it would be that I always understand what my relationship is to the land. One of the things that's most difficult about the way I'm traveling now, doing readings and all, is that I have to go in and out of places so fast I don't get to look at where I am. It's spiritually disruptive.

There's a power that accrues to writers and artists in our culture, a mystique of fame. I'm thinking of that woman you write about in one of your essays who recognizes you at a radio station and asks you, "What's it like to be a star?" You seemed surprised at her remark.

I wasn't surprised, but I was disconcerted and upset because I don't think about my writing as being about fame: I think of it in a communal context. Yet it's naive and apolitical to deny that elements of privilege accrue to visibility. Certainly, a visibly lesbian artist is doing something that many lesbians can't do in their own work lives. That visibility is the result of community building, of something that is given to the lesbian artist from the lesbian community. When I think about these issues, it seems all the more reason to be scrupulous about how to return things to the community and to place my life in perspective. I've worked hard, but I certainly could not be doing this by myself. The other thing I know about power is what I've learned from Audre Lorde, who said that if we don't use our power, it will be turned against us. I think there is an important distinction between power over and power with. I'm interested in how we develop power with others. I think it's important that my having access to my own power in my writing doesn't mean draining it away from the community or using it in opposition to others but, rather, using my power collectively with others to build a transformative future.

(1992)

May Miller Sullivan

May Miller Sullivan turned to writing poetry after a long career as a teacher and playwright. She was born in 1899 in Washington, D.C., and was raised on the campus of Howard University, where her father, Kelly Miller, was a dean and professor. Sullivan was exposed to numerous notable African-American leaders, educators, artists, and writers while growing up. She attended Howard University, earning her bachelor's degree in 1920. Sullivan became one of the most renowned and most published playwrights of the Harlem Renaissance. During the last two decades, some of her plays have been restaged, and some have been published for the first time. Her last play, *Freedom's Children on the March* (1943), was performed at the Frederick Douglass High School, where she had taught for several years. Her books of poetry include *Collected Poetry* (1989), *The Clearing and Beyond* (1974), *Halfway to the Sun* (1981), and *The Ransomed Wait* (1983).

He has yet to meet our phantom
while we unmask the beast
to learn that total lack of fear
and freedom from guilt
an ultimate innocence
belonging only to the young
where no past nuzzles
       ("The Edge of Return")

What is the significance of these lines?

There are two factions in each of us—one hopeful, one always questioning. The conflict within creates a dramatic tension between the two selves. We must understand where we come from before we can go forward.

What kind of concerns motivate your poetry?

How small the planet is in the universe, how the individual has a measured time in the moving world and must contribute to the welfare of not a single situation, person, or race but of all humankind.

Why do you think your poems express not simple optimism but sustained hope for a better world?

I was greatly influenced by my father's view that, despite the days of slavery and suffering, there is hope for the future. We must reach out and extend toward the hope of progress even if it's never fully within our grasp.

The use and misuse of the universe seems to be a recurrent theme in your poems.

When I wrote "Tally," my first major publication, I had read in the paper about the explosion of the nuclear bomb, and I sat at my coffee table that night and thought: "What's going to become of human beings? What must a woman be feeling who, at this time, is conceiving a child? Wouldn't she feel maybe it was better that the seed be lost in some 'clearer stream / to lap some lonely lighthouse rock / Or green again the passing plain.'" When that poem was published I sent it to H. L. Mencken, who said: "A fine piece of stuff. I'm glad you had it published."

How about your recent poem "Anemones"?

I wrote it after reading an article in the *Washington Post* that stated that the world had come from nothing and to nothing may return, and I thought, "What are we doing to hurry that about?" We aren't satisfied with letting nature take its course. Political movements lose sight of a thing that is larger than politics—the rights of humankind.

Where does the influence of science and astronomy come from in your poems?

We associated all the classics with the stars in the heavens. My father studied astronomy at Johns Hopkins in the 1890s and taught us the history of the cosmos as children. I remember going out in the garden, and my father pointed out Halley's comet—it must have been 1910. I recall saying, "Oh, yes." I don't know whether I saw it or whether I imagined I saw it. We knew all the planets and the constellations. My first poem (at fourteen) was a god-awful one to Venus the goddess of love. It was published in *School Progress Magazine,* and they sent me a check for twenty-five cents.

Did you want to be a poet at that time?

Oh no, I wanted to be a dancer. We went to a dancing class and the Howard Theatre. I wanted to be the girl at the end of the chorus line kicking up my heels.

Was that ever a possibility?

Of course not! My father expected all five of us to go to college. We were all Howard graduates. At that time you followed the schedule worked out by your parents.

Your dramatic training is evident in the way you organize your readings. How do you communicate with audiences both young and old?

In any form of art we have to consider our readers and our listeners. I realize the value of the dramatic element in capturing the audience's attention. No matter how intricate a poem may be, you want to share its meaning and get the audience involved. When I studied theater at Columbia University, we learned that the presentation is the real test of the material. A recent event featured my children's book, *Halfway to the Sun,* which takes its title from "Hummingbird": "Bird tinier than my thumb / I could wish wings for me / strong as yours for you / to dare the mystery of space / halfway to the sun." We talked about people working together, and I told them that nobody has solved the mystery of how all this came about but we are a race of human beings and we have to save the earth, not help destroy it. We won't all be on the front page; that isn't the point. The point is to give the best that's in you, and that's all anyone can ask.

Your poetry is in a way a capsule history of the twentieth century, for example, "April Parable": "April whipped the air to prophecy / Man will end war or war man." Or "Blazing Accusations," on the children's death in the Atlanta church bombing: "Too early a death for those who young / have lost prophecy in blast and flame." How can we stop violence and wanton destruction?

The solution is much greater than I am. I can't create a permanent solution. The only thing I know is my feeling as a lone woman. My hope is that someone will read or hear a poem of mine and say, "She seeks the truth," and respond to it.

Your children's poems are songs of innocence, the others, songs of experience—shades of William Blake.

I like that.

I am struck by your ability to integrate life and art and the way your poems meditate on mortality—your own and that of all human beings.

I got the feeling when I was a child that we were all one. I can recall my father saying, "Remember Africa has its tradition, but when it meets another culture it goes beyond that African background, yet we carry it within us too." He had a great belief in the promise of the future and told us man would walk on the moon; I'm sorry he never lived to see it. My children's poem, "Skywriting," uses the Southern folk legend that the man in the moon was imprisoned there for burning brush on the seventh day. The nose was the man; the mouth was the fire. My sister complained that it ruined her fantasy when man reached the moon, but I never felt that way.

What in your own life is true to your values?

I'm happy that I came up without prejudice. We grew up in the [integrated] Howard community on College Street. I consider the lines from a poem of my father's a moral axiom, "And those who love the self same thing / Must therefore one another love."

Have you ever felt discriminated against as a woman or as a Black woman?

No, maybe I have seen some situations that have been almost ugly. I always felt, well, look here, I'm above that. You can't hurt me. There isn't any way in the world that you are going to diminish me because I'm a black woman.

What made you start writing plays?

I was influenced by Montgomery Gregory and Alain Locke at Howard. I won the first drama prize at graduation. Afterwards, we staged one-act plays at Morgan College, and Carter Woodson [founder, the Association for the Study of Negro Life and History] suggested that I write about Negro heroines. That was when I wrote my plays about Sojourner Truth and Harriet Tubman.

Did you get any other recognition for your plays?

The Bog Guide won a prize in the First Opportunity contest in New York in 1925, the same year that Langston Hughes and Countee Cullen won for poetry and Zora Neale Hurston for fiction. [Eugene O'Neill, Alexander Woolcott, Montgomery Gregory, and Robert Benchley were the judges for drama.]

What about recently?

I won the National Society Mr. Brown award for excellence in theater from the African Company in New York in 1986. The irony is that that award came more than forty years after I shifted from drama to poetry.

Why do your plays, unlike your poetry, make more use of folk idiom?

When I studied with Frederic Koch at Columbia, he stressed the need to preserve and interpret the folk tradition. He taught us that when you're using folk material you should come as close as possible to folk idiom. When my play "Riding the Goat" [recommended for high school use] was labeled "offensive" by the *Afro American,* I said, "I have no scruples against using the word *nigger* or any of the words we taboo when portraying a character who in life uses them."

What women poets have influenced you?

Inez Boulton, who was Harriet Monroe's assistant at *Poetry,* influenced and helped me most. She introduced me to many of the outstanding writers who visited her: Thornton Wilder, Anaïs Nin, Elizabeth Bishop, and Gwendolyn Brooks. That's how Gwendolyn and I first became friends. The first recognized black woman poet who encouraged me was Georgia Douglas Johnson. She was of my father's generation and wrote like Sara Teasdale. My father, W. E. B. Du Bois, James Weldon Johnson, Jean Toomer, Langston Hughes when he was in town, the whole crowd hung out at her Saturday night gatherings. And, of course, Josephine Jacobsen, who wrote the introduction to *Lyrics of Three Women* and invited me to record at the Library of Congress. You keep writing and hope that critical reaction will be positive. That is why I was so gratified that Josephine said *The Ransomed Wait* contained the strongest poems I'd written.

What women poets from the past do you admire?

Emily Dickinson. We all admire her because she wrote the truth from a woman's viewpoint. The more I read her, the more I wonder how she had the courage to write as she did, when she did. She had a freedom of spirit despite the restrictions on women in her time.

How do you view the role of women?

I have always felt that women must have self-expression more than just carrying the seed, although one of the sorrows of my life is that I never had children. I needed to go beyond the established bounds of a woman's role, which is why I turned to writing—to gain personal fulfillment and because I couldn't stay home and stare at four walls.

(1987)

Photo by David Gottlieb

Karen Swenson

Karen Swenson, poet and journalist, was born in New York City in 1936. The awards and honors Swenson has received include the Ann Stanford Poetry Award, a Yaddo fellowship, an Albee Foundation fellowship, and the National Poetry Series in 1993. Her third book, *The Landlady in Bangkok* (1994), was chosen by Maxine Kumin as winner of the National Poetry Prize. Swenson has traveled extensively, particularly through the Far East, and has written many travel articles.

How does the "Old women ought to be explorers" epigraph resonate with your own experience as a woman and a poet?

Tyros reinvent the wheel. You need to know before you are ready to explore. The best exploration is based on a foundation of knowledge and experience. That's true of both intellectual and physical exploration.

It took me many years of writing in free verse to become ready to investigate form, meter, rhyme. And it took many years of writing confessionally before I ventured out beyond self and family. My life experiences moved me along that trajectory—having a child, divorcing (both birth experiences), and being an itinerant poet. In youth it is so important to belong, to be part of. Later, one can become interested in being apart from, in being different. Although I felt more alien as a young woman than I do now.

Certainly, you were an alien in Asia, both ethnically and culturally. What was that like?

It was freeing. In one's own society one is always imprisoned by the culture's rules. To be alien is to be outside the rules. That, of course, isn't really true, since actually you become subject to a new set of rules, and, to make it trickier, you usually don't know what they are. In 1974 I went to Iran, taking my twelve-year-old son along as protection. (It's one thing to travel alone as a "woman" and something quite different to travel as a "mother," particularly in a Muslim country.) Men were so astonished by my lonely presence on buses and in teahouses they decided to treat me like a man. Although occasionally inconvenient, it was certainly better than being treated like a Muslim woman.

Being alien magnificently wrenches me out of my culture, gives me a chance to view what we take for granted as much as breathing, to see it from a different perspective, test its values, see if I agree. Many Western or American cultural beliefs range from repulsive to silly. The Thais, for instance, make very little fuss about sexual preference. You should produce children; after, it's your problem. It is so much more sensible than our hysterical insistence on heterosexuality.

An advantage for women who travel alone is the exhilaration of sloughing off, like snake skin, our "at home" roles—daughter, wife, mother—which leaves us a little naked and very much a mystery to ourselves and others. Another advantage is that we, more than men, are responsible for our surroundings. We often do home maintenance for a living, so what delight to be in a hotel room, responsible for nothing—bed, sink, or husband's breakfast.

Although you claim "old womanhood" as a position from which to write, the writer you are today must have origins further back. Was there something in your background, your childhood, that created the poet?

My mother read poetry to me: not just nursery rhymes but Frost and Masefield. She had a real feeling for words. She enjoyed the sound of them in her mouth, their possibilities, putting them together so that they startled. On long drives she would recite huge hunks of "Hiawatha," thumping the rhythm out with her palm on the steering wheel. She thought it was a howl and would declaim in ranting style. Everyone but the cat and dog in our house went to bed with a book, and when I was fifteen and living with my aunt Liz in Mexico I was allowed—oh joy—to read at the dining room table.

If pain makes poets, I had my portion. My mother was a batterer, and my father was an active alcoholic, as I was for many years. The description of what I saw became important to me early on. I grew up believing that relationships and events could be altered through communication.

When did you know that you were a poet?

I had rigid ideas about what constituted a poet and would not say I was one, although I would say I wrote, until I was published. Thinking that way caused me trouble. Early in my career I went for long periods between getting published, which set me up for believing I was no longer a poet as well as for a feeling of failure. I did not come from people who thought you could become a poet by deciding to be one or by doing the work involved. You had to have confirmation from the outside. To my parents you were what the world said you were. This caused them, and me, much unhappiness.

What has kept you writing all these years?

It certainly wasn't encouragement. I suspect I actually like to write, although I have managed to hide this fact from myself for many years. My Germanic background dictates that you should not like what you do—anything else would be despicable self-indulgence. I also kept going because the task itself is so enthrallingly complex.

In terms of poetry and meaning, what is it that you do when you write poems?

A poem often starts as an unattached image—like the betel box in "The Cambodian Box." As I write, I reveal to myself why that image is important to me. For me the basis of all art is communication. An electrician is an expert on the wiring in my house; I am his expert on the communication of emotion and meaning. The artist has always been the fountainhead of significance in any culture. An artist attempts to express an understanding of life within the given cultural guidelines, and, if the guidelines are inadequate in some way, you break through them. Emily Dickinson certainly did that.

I'm not sure when or why meaning began to leak out of Western culture. Perhaps it was the loss of God or the Industrial Revolution and the separation from the land, but accompanying that drain has been the loss of ordinary people's interest in art. Art has become a specialty, like ophthalmic surgery—too complex, too abstruse, for the average reader or viewer. This, in turn, has caused art to move away from people and toward institutions. Poetry became a school lesson, separate from fun or beauty or excitement. Paintings began to appear in corporate headquarters. Devoid of meaning, a painting will offend no one; it will merely show how cultured, well meaning, or rich Exxon is. Exxon is not going to hang Munch's painting *The Scream* in corporate headquarters.

I feel, as is apparent in "We," that my responsibility is to investigate the significance of things. I don't mean that I am looking for a moral, but I am looking for the connection between people, between the world and us. I feel the best writers do this—Linda Hogan, for instance. This increases the risks I take, since the reader may not agree with my meaning or like it. I can be wrong. Trying to elucidate significance may make me sentimental, spiteful, or judgmental. There are a lot of things to trip over once you get involved with meaning. I want a poem to be beautiful, but I also want it to be involved in the world of ideas and emotions.

So how does a poem—let's take "The Cambodian Box" as an example—get itself onto the page? What is the experience of writing the poem as you live it?

I brought a silver betel box in Bangkok in the form of a pair of geese nestled in a basket—I recognized the work as Cambodian. It was an exquisite little sculpture, each feather distinctly etched and the lovely roundness of the geese. I began to track it backwards, to think about how and why it had come into my possession. A woman or man had tucked it, perhaps with others, into a sarong or bag and run from the Khmer Rouge, Pol Pot.

The West's tendency to see good and evil as separate entities rather than as connected paradoxes has always seemed to me one of the great weaknesses of our philosophical and religious thinking. It is, to me, quite apparently untrue. I find the East attractive because there opposites are integral to each other. The little betel box seemed to me to be an example of this paradox of human skill in creation and destruction, of beauty and torture. These are the opposing kinds of craftsmanship of which we are capable.

Your last book, A Sense of Direction, *contains poem after poem that is deeply personal. Was your subject when that book was written different from your subject today?*

I doubt that I have that kind of overview of my work. I would guess, however, that the details have changed from personal to cultural, while the obsessions have stayed the same. Certainly, the role of women is an obsession in my first book [*An Attic of Ideals*], in *A Sense of Direction*, and in *Landlady*. The importance of accepting responsibility for one's actions is as present in "The White Rabbit" as in "We."

At one point in your career, when a budget crunch left you jobless, you made a clear decision to live by poetry, becoming what you have called "an itinerant poet." What did that choice cost you, and what did it give you?

It cost me a Ph.D. degree in Old English and made my son, I fear, feel abandoned, but I gained a new sense of self and an intimate knowledge of parts of my country I would not otherwise have seen. Traveling is for me, always, a spiritual journey. I spent six years driving in the Rockies, where it always seemed to be February. I was told in a southern Colorado town, where I was doing Poets in the Schools work: "We don't have trouble with Anglos here. We don't have any Anglos here." It was the beginning of my travel, the start of my confrontation with my fears.

My journeys also gave me glimpses of other people's lives that shook me out of the "quiet tenor" of my ways. In that same southern Colorado town I taught a young man, the most talented high school student I had ever been lucky enough to encounter. I noticed that he had three deep scars on his cheek. I couldn't imagine what they were from. I asked his teacher, who told me with no sense of oddness: "In seventh grade he decided he was an atheist, and therefore he had to be scarred. He makes the wounds with his razor and keeps them open."

As poet and teacher, how did you perceive those scars at the time?

With horror at the lack of understanding on the part of the community that surrounded him. I tried to see that he would get into college. He refused to take the SATs. When I returned to that town, he wouldn't come to school while I was there. The whole incident broke my heart—that such talent should behave so punitively toward itself—but that is what a mercantile culture frequently does to art.

In Landlady *you quote Eric Fromm, "Evilness is specifically human phenomenon." Why did you choose that line?*

Evil has always been with us. In the West we have seen it from various angles over the centuries, as sin, as psychosis—we have moved from thinking of it as something willed to something uncontrolled. That, I think, is progress. It is specifically human because evil requires consciousness. A cat is cruel to a mouse by our standards, but the cat has no consciousness, therefore, no empathy, and, therefore, cruel doesn't exist for a cat. Knowledge of good and evil presupposes an ability to imagine oneself as both victim and victimizer.

When governments want to make their people into consciousness killers, the first thing they do is to dehumanize the enemy and make people afraid. What you dehumanize and what you fear you remove from the arena of empathy. Words help: *Gook, Kike*. When you live in horror of being killed, it is much easier to kill.

In the individual torturer or sex criminal, as in your ordinary person, the lineage is from victim to victim. Alice Miller has worked this out magnificently in her books. If you have been victimized, you will victimize. The eleven-year-old who killed the fourteen-year-old who was, in turn, killed by his gang has cigarette burns all over his body because he had been tortured as a child. You cannot expect children to be nice children or adults if you burn them with cigarettes. Evil is just a hand-me-down from father to son, from mother to daughter.

(1995)

Janet Palmer Mullaney is founding editor and publisher of *Belles Lettres: A Review of Books by Women.* She received the Bookwoman of the Year Award from the Library of Congress, an award whose previous recipients include Eleanor Roosevelt, Pearl Buck, and Rachel Carson. **Toi Derricotte** is a poet and teacher of poetry. Her most recent books are *Invisible Dreams: Poems of Embodiment,* a poetry collection, and *The Black Notebooks,* a literary memoir. She has been the recipient of numerous awards, including fellowships from the National Endowment for the Arts, the Pioneering in the Arts Award from National Black Artists Inc., and the Pushcart Prize.